X

Twayne's English Authors Series

Sylvia E. Bowman, *Editor*

INDIANA UNIVERSITY

D. H. Lawrence

 7

D. H. Lawrence

By RONALD P. DRAPER

University of Leicester, England

TWAYNE PUBLISHERS

A DIVISION OF G. K. HALL & CO., BOSTON

PR
6003
.A93
Z624

823.912
LAW
D
1964

−M 2− 12/82   Pub. 10,16

To My Wife

Contents

Preface

Since the publication in America of *The Achievement of D. H. Lawrence* (edited by Frederick J. Hoffman and Harry T. Moore, 1953) and in England of F. R. Leavis' *D. H. Lawrence, Novelist* (1955), criticism of Lawrence has swung away from the personal involvement that vitiated so much earlier commentary to concentrate instead on the actual work that he wrote. One recent book (by Eliseo Vivas) specifically tries to discriminate between "the failure and the triumph" of Lawrence's "art." This is a wholly admirable and sane redressing of the balance. Lawrence is now an accepted major writer—with W. B. Yeats and T. S. Eliot, I should say, he is one of the three most important writers in English in the twentieth century—and it is fitting that his work should be accorded the same *critical* treatment that is given to other major writers. Moreover, Lawrence's own famous dictum—"Never trust the artist. Trust the tale. The proper function of a critic is to save the tale from the artist who created it."—should also be applied to his own work. Lawrence is read, and will continue to be, for his novels, tales, and poems; and these must be preserved, not only from injudicious admirers and detractors, but, where necessary, from the misrepresentations that derive from Lawrence's own didactic rather than artistic self.

Yet it would be a mistake to assume that Lawrence's work can be dissociated from his life. He is a very different writer from, say, Chaucer, or the Renaissance "maker" such as Spenser. Donne, or Milton, or Wordsworth—writers whose life and work "interinanimate" one another—provide better parallels, though the connection is even more intimate with Lawrence. What he says of his poems can, with some qualification, be said of all his writings: ". . . they make up a biography of an emotional and inner life." And each one "needs the penumbra of its own time and place and circumstances to make it full and whole," for Lawrence's method of listening honestly and attentively to the voice that speaks within him at the moment precludes the kind of art that is the extracted essence of the whole of the artist's experience. This point should not, however, be pushed too far. Of *The Rainbow* and *Women in Love* it *can* be said that Lawrence is attempting a fully integrated interpretation of his experience which exists quite apart from the particular person, time, and place which generated it—though, even so, the value of knowing something about Lawrence's personal history is obvious. But, in general, it is true that the life and the work must be read together, and partly as commentaries on one another.

The aim of the present study is to try to meet both these requirements in the reading of Lawrence—the consideration of his work as self-substantial art, and the recognition of its "relativity." The first chapter deals with the influence of his home and Nottinghamshire environment and with the "search for a lost Atlantis" which underlies his nomadic wanderings over Europe, Australia, and America. The remaining chapters analyze his novels, tales, and poems, primarily as works of art, but bearing in mind, as a kind of intermittent running commentary, the relationship which they have to his life and to the rest of his work.

I have frequently quoted from Lawrence's own comments in his letters and elsewhere, believing that an author should be allowed to speak for himself as much as possible. I have also taken the liberty of contradicting him where my own critical judgment has impelled me to do so. I profoundly admire and respect Lawrence, but I cannot always agree with him; and, where this is the case, I have tried to say so plainly and, I hope, without arrogating to myself a superior wisdom.

R. P. DRAPER

University of Leicester,
England

Acknowledgments

I wish to extend my grateful acknowledgments to The Viking Press, Inc., New York and to Alfred A. Knopf, Inc., New York for permission to quote from the works of D. H. Lawrence. The Viking Press publishes the following works: *Aaron's Rod; Amores; Apocalypse; The Boy in the Bush; The Captain's Doll; Collected Poems; Collected Letters; England, My England; Etruscan Places; Fantasia of the Unconscious; Kangaroo; Last Poems; The Letters of D. H. Lawrence; Look! We Have Come Through!; The Lost Girl; Love Among the Haystacks; The Lovely Lady; A Modern Lover; New Poems; Phoenix; The Prussian Officer; Psychoanalysis and the Unconscious; The Rainbow; Sea and Sardinia; Sons and Lovers; Studies in Classic American Literature; Touch and Go; Twilight in Italy; The Widowing of Mrs. Holroyd; Women in Love.* Alfred A. Knopf publishes: *Assorted Articles; David; The Man Who Died; Mornings in Mexico; The Plumed Serpent; Pornography and Obscenity; St. Mawr; The Woman Who Rode Away; The Virgin and the Gipsy.* Acknowledgments are also due to the Estate of the late Mrs. Frieda Lawrence and Laurence Pollinger Limited for permission to quote from *The White Peacock* and *The Trespasser* and to the Estate of the late Mrs. Frieda Lawrence, Laurence Pollinger Limited, and also Alfred A. Knopf, Inc. for permission to quote from *Lady Chatterley's Lover*. In addition, I should like to thank Mr. Stephen Spender for permission to quote from *World Within World;* Professor Richard Hoggart and the editors of *The Critical Quarterly* for permission to quote from "A Question of Tone" (*C. Q.*, Spring, 1963); and the editors of *The Critical Quarterly* for permitting me to make use of my article on "Authority and the Individual: A Study of D. H. Lawrence's *Kangaroo*" (*C. Q.*, Autumn, 1959).

I should also like to take this opportunity to express my admiration for, and sense of indebtedness to, the Lawrence scholarship of Harry T. Moore and Edward Nehls; and I hope the many other authors of books wholly or partially about Lawrence on whose work I have drawn will accept this general acknowledgment of my gratitude and debt to them. To Sylvia Bowman, the editor of this series, I am indebted for much patient correction of my original manuscript, and to my wife I am grateful for sympathy, advice, and continual assistance.

Chronology

1885   September 11—David Herbert Richards Lawrence born at Eastwood, Nottinghamshire, fourth child of Arthur Lawrence, a miner, and Lydia Lawrence (*née* Beardsall), formerly a schoolteacher.

1898   Won a scholarship to the Nottingham Boys' High School.

1901   Lawrence's brother, William Ernest Lawrence (the "William" of *Sons and Lovers*) died. Lawrence met Jessie Chambers (the "Miriam" of *Sons and Lovers*) at the Haggs. In the summer, he obtained a job with a Nottingham manuacturer of surgical appliances. Left when he suffered first serious attack of pneumonia.

1902–   Uncertified teacher, first at Eastwood, then at Ilkeston.
1906

1906   Began two-year teacher-training course at University College, Nottingham.

1907   Some time during this year he began *The White Peacock*.

1908   October 12, took post as schoolmaster at Davidson Road Boys' School, Croydon, South London.

1909   Through Jessie Chambers, had first poems accepted and published (November) in the *English Review*. Met its editor, Ford Madox Ford. August, holiday on the Isle of Wight (remembered in *The Trespasser*).

1910   *The White Peacock* accepted by Heinemann (published in January, 1911). Working on *The Trespassers* and early form of *Sons and Lovers*. Mother died of cancer, December 9.

1911   Ill in November, gave up teaching.

1912   *The Trespasser* published. April, met Frieda Weekley, wife of Professor of French at University College, Nottingham (Frieda second daughter of Baron Friedrich von Richthofen—born August 11, 1879—married Ernest Weekley,

1899—three children). Eloped with Frieda in May. Walked over Tyrolese Alps. Spent winter at Gargnano, Lago di Garda (scene of much of *Twilight in Italy*).

1913　*Love Poems and Others* and *Sons and Lovers* published. Working on *The Sisters* (later split into *The Rainbow* and *Women in Love*).

1914　*The Prussian Officer* published. Frieda obtained divorce, married Lawrence, July 13. Lawrence on walking tour of Lakes when war declared. Toyed with idea of idealistic colony (Rananim).

1915　*The Rainbow* published in September, suppressed November 13. Frieda and Lawrence spent latter part of year in Cornwall. Met Lady Ottoline Morrell (later to appear in *Women in Love* as Hermione).

1916–
1917　Mainly in Cornwall. Finished *Women in Love*. Medically examined in June, 1917, for war service, but found unfit. October, expelled from Cornwall on suspicion of spying (recalled in *Kangaroo*).

1918–
1919　September, further medical examination. Beginning of 1919 seriously ill with influenza. October, Frieda went to Germany, Lawrence to Florence, via Turin (*cf. Aaron's Rod*). Reunited, they went to Capri, via Picinisco (*cf.* last part of *The Lost Girl*).

1920　Private edition of *Women in Love* published in New York in May. *The Lost Girl* published in November. Most of the year spent in Italy and Taormina, Sicily. Many of his best poems written.

1921　Awarded James Tait Black prize for *The Lost Girl*. January, made the excursion to Sardinia recorded in *Sea and Sardinia* (published in December). Wrote more poems, "The Captain's Doll," and finished *Aaron's Rod*.

1922　*Aaron's Rod* published in April. *Fantasia of the Unconscious* and *England, My England* published, October, both in New York. Increasingly occupied with idea of going to America. Set out for Ceylon (*cf.* poem, "Elephant"), then on to Australia. At Perth met Molly Skinner with whom later collaborated on *The Boy in the Bush*, and in New South Wales stayed from May to August at "Wyewurk," Thirroul, where *Kangaroo* was written. By September in Taos, New Mexico. Mixed reactions, as in American essays.

1923–　March, went to Mexico City. April—July, Lake Chapala,

1924   Mexico, working on *The Plumed Serpent*. August, New York. Frieda wanted to return to England, Lawrence did not. Quarreled and Frieda sailed without him. Lawrence went back to Mexico, but in November sailed to rejoin her. In London the "Last Supper" fiasco took place—Lawrence invited various friends to revive Rananim with him, overdrank, and passed out. After visits to France and Germany returned to Taos, and then went on, in November, to Oaxaca, Mexico, where continued work on *The Plumed Serpent*.

1925   Finished *The Plumed Serpent*. Seriously ill with "malaria," had to leave Oaxaca. Recuperated at the New Mexico ranch. In September returned to Europe. *St. Mawr* published in May.

1926– This period spent mainly at the Villa Mirenda, Florence,
1927   with intervening visits to Germany and England. Did some painting and worked seriously at *Lady Chatterley's Lover* (three versions). March–April, 1927, with Earl Brewster made a walking tour of Etruscan tombs and museums out of which *Etruscan Places* came. *The Plumed Serpent* published, January, 1926.

1928   January, third version of *Lady Chatterley* completed. *The Woman Who Rode Away* published in May. *Lady Chatterley*, Florence edition, July.

1929   Exhibition of Lawrence's paintings held in London, raided by police in July (see the amusing "Innocent England"). Wintered at Bandol, working on *Last Poems*.

1930   February 6, entered "Ad Astra" sanatorium, Vence, France. March 1, moved to Villa Robermond. March 2, died.

1935   Ashes taken to New Mexico.

CHAPTER 1

Introduction

I *The Setting*

D. H. LAWRENCE was born in 1885 at Eastwood, a mining village in Nottinghamshire. The date and the place are both important. Nottinghamshire is a roughly oval-shaped county, bordering in the east on the low-lying, agricultural lands of Lincolnshire, and in the west on the hilly industrial area of Derbyshire. The city of Nottingham lies in the southern part of the county where the River Trent makes a wide southward curve before flowing north to the Humber and the sea. Eastwood, eight miles northwest of the city, stands on a hill overlooking the Erewash valley which carries the main railway line to London, and also forms the border between the counties of Nottinghamshire and Derbyshire.

The region to which the village belongs is thus one of contrasts and connections. Unlike the Lake District of Wordsworth, or the Dorset of Hardy, the area is neither isolated nor homogeneous; and Lawrence, much as he has in common with his two great predecessors in the Romantic and regionalist traditions, is not a writer whose mind was formed by the pressures of a permanent and unchanging environment remote from the major centers of population and major social upheavals of his day. On the contrary, his birthplace is at the very heart of England. His native area, "the country of my heart," as he describes it in a letter to Rolf Gardiner, is to him "real England—the hard pith of England." [1] And Lawrence himself is almost quintessentially English: "And I am English," he writes in another letter, "and my Englishness is my very vision." [2] But he came to detest his home and his country because of his experiences during World War I and also because of the alternate neglect and contempt with which his most serious work was treated by his countrymen. But, as that work abundantly proves, he never escaped, nor did he fundamentally want to escape, the influence of his native region.

In "Nottingham and the Mining Countryside," which together with his fictionalized autobiography, *Sons and Lovers,* provides the most important information that we have about his early environment, Lawrence at the age of forty-three looks back on the area where he was born, and comments:

> To me it seemed, and still seems, an extremely beautiful country-side, just between the red sandstone and the oak-trees of Nottingham, and the cold limestone, the ash-trees, the stone fences of Derbyshire. To me, as a child and a young man, it was still the old England of the forest and agricultural past; there were no motor-cars, the mines were, in a sense, an accident in the landscape, and Robin Hood and his merry men were not very far away.[3]

The life of the old agricultural England, with its rhythm based on the natural cycle of the seasons, still persisted; but the influence of the Industrial Revolution of the nineteenth century had penetrated deep. "Somewhere about 1820," writes Lawrence, "the company must have sunk the first big shaft" which started the change from mines that were no more than "an accident in the landscape" to "the real industrial colliery."[4] These new mines were a blight on the countryside, accompanied as they were by ugly pit-heads, artificial hills of slag-heaps, dingy back-to-back houses, "dull little shops,"[5] and the bare public houses where the miners spent their evenings talking and drinking beer.

According to his lifelong friend, William Hopkin, "From his early days Lawrence had a great love for nature and the country-side. It was a delight to go rambling with him."[6] Jessie Chambers (the Miriam of *Sons and Lovers*) also bears testimony to his love of the countryside; and, through her and her parents and brothers who farmed the Haggs (about two miles north of Eastwood), he acquired an intimate firsthand knowledge of farm life. (In a letter to one of the Chambers brothers written in 1928 from France, he says nostalgically: "Whatever I forget, I shall never forget the Haggs—I loved it so. . . . whatever else I am, I am somewhere still the same Bert who rushed with such joy to the Haggs."[7])

The industrialism which scarred the countryside and altered the very texture of ordinary life was, therefore, felt particularly keenly by Lawrence: "The real tragedy of England, as I see it, is the tragedy of ugliness. The country is so lovely: the man-made England is so vile."[8] And "tragedy" is not used here journalistically, for Lawrence means much more than that something aesthetically pleasing to the eye has been spoilt. With the ugliness goes an impoverishment of the quality of life, a hard, raw insentience, communicated, for example, in the description of Tevershall (which is Eastwood, of course) in the following passage from *Lady Chatterley's Lover:*

> The car ploughed uphill through the long squalid straggle of Tevershall, the blackened brick dwellings, the black slate roofs glistening their sharp edges, the mud black with coal dust, the pavements wet and black. It was as if dismalness had soaked through and through everything. The utter negation of natural beauty, the utter negation of the gladness of life, the utter absence of the instinct for shapely beauty which every bird and beast has, the utter death of the human intuitive faculty was appalling. The stacks of soap in the grocers' shops, the rhubarb and lemons in the greengrocers'! the awful hats in the milliners'! all went by ugly, ugly, ugly, followed by the plaster-and-gilt horror of the cinema with its wet picture announcements, 'A Woman's Love!', and the new big Primitive chapel, primitive enough in its stark brick and big panes of greenish and raspberry glass in the windows. The Wesleyan chapel, higher up, was of blackened brick and stood behind iron railings and blackened shrubs. The Congregational chapel, which thought itself superior, was built of rusticated sandstone and had a steeple, but not a very high one. Just beyond were the new school buildings, expensive pink brick, and gravelled playground inside iron railings, all very imposing, and mixing the suggestion of a chapel and a prison. Standard Five girls were having a singing lesson, just finishing the la-me-do-la exercises and beginning a 'sweet children's song.' Anything more unlike song, spontaneous song, would be impossible to imagine: a strange bawling yell that followed the outlines of a tune. It was not like savages: savages have subtle rhythms. It was not like animals: animals *mean* something when they yell. It was like nothing on earth, and it was called singing. Connie sat and listened with her heart in her boots, as Field was filling petrol. What could possibly become of such a people, a people in whom the living intuitive faculty was dead as nails, and only queer mechanical yells and uncanny will-power remained? (Chap. 11)

Both the essay, "Nottingham and the Mining Countryside" and the novel, *Lady Chatterley's Lover,* belong to the last years of Lawrence's life which he spent mainly in Italy. The sheer lack of form in the typical English mining village (which Eastwood is) and the typical English city (which Nottingham is) struck him more forcefully then than it had done earlier. It drew him to the conclusion that the English, who had been a rural people till

1800, when they found themselves herded into large new centers of population by the demands of industry, failed to develop an urban, or civic, sense. Siena, though small, was a real city: Nottingham "sprawling" and "an amorphous agglomeration." [9] In his "Autobiographical Fragment" (which is really a piece of Utopianism in the spirit of William Morris' *News from Nowhere*), he imagines Eastwood transformed into a brave new city, the antithesis of Connie's Tevershall:

> And at the top of the hill was a town, all yellow in the late afternoon light, with yellow, curved walls rising massive from the yellow-leaved orchards, and above, buildings swerving in a long, oval curve, and round, faintly conical towers rearing up. It had something at once soft and majestical about it, with its soft yet powerful curves, and no sharp angles or edges, the whole substance seeming soft and golden like the golden flesh of a city.[10]

But this fragment, too, is a late work. His sense of the contrast between the reality of Eastwood and what it might have been was sharpened by his experience of other places, but much more importantly by his own fully developed ideas about the nature of man and his connection with all the various nonhuman forms of life. The inwardness of his earlier understanding has gone—though it comes back to him occasionally. In *Sons and Lovers* and in *The Rainbow*, he is still very close to the experience as he lived through it. In particular, the people of his region, though they possess some of the characteristics that he gives to them in *Lady Chatterley's Lover*, are seen much less from the point of view of a man who has made up his mind. This is not to say that the later work in which Lawrence reverts to the Nottinghamshire and Derbyshire background fails to tell the truth but that it is less able to communicate the whole truth, since by then Lawrence has crystallized his intuitions into doctrine which forms a mold for his experience. The great novels of the first phase of his maturity as a novelist (excluding the early work in which he is a youthful experimenter) are explorations of his experience from which the doctrines later emerge. Lawrence, who recognized this development, stated it quite frankly in the Foreword to *Fantasia of the Unconscious:*

> This pseudo-philosophy of mine—'pollyanalytics,' as one of my respected critics might say—is deduced from the novels and poems, not

the reverse. The novels and poems come unwatched out of one's pen. And then the absolute need which one has for some sort of satisfactory mental attitude towards oneself and things in general makes one try to abstract some definite conclusions from one's experiences as a writer and as a man. The novels and poems are pure passionate experience. These 'pollyanalytics' are inferences made afterwards, from the experience.

The conscious formulations, and those of the later works most under their spell, are not, therefore, to be ignored. On the contrary, they are still works of considerable importance that would earn Lawrence a major place in English literature even if their greater predecessors were unknown, and they are also frequently the most valuable commentary that we have on the earlier work.

II *The Family*

The contrasts which form such a striking feature of the area in which Lawrence was brought up are even more evident in his domestic background. His father, Arthur Lawrence, a miner, and his mother, Lydia Beardsall, who had been a schoolteacher in the southeast, were sharply opposed types. According to Harry T. Moore, this difference is exaggerated by Lawrence, especially in the comic-satiric poem, "Red Herring." His father had a lower middle-class background and was related by marriage to Lydia Beardsall's family. Nevertheless, Lawrence's home was working-class, with all that that meant in an England then rigidly divided into separate classes. There was a painful tension between the husband who truculently asserted his workman's status ("he was always saying tiresome and foolish things about the men just above him in control at the mine. He offended them all, almost on purpose"), and the wife, conscious of her origins in "the lower bourgeoisie," who "spoke King's English, without an accent, and never in her life could even imitate a sentence of the dialect which my father spoke, and which we children spoke out of doors." [11]

The clash of personalities between them was certainly strong, as both Lawrence and Ada, his sister, bear witness. The mother loved reading and was visited by the local minister with whom she talked religion and philosophy. "She was never effusive or demonstrative in any way," and she was "a stickler for truth, having great contempt for anything petty, vain or frivolous." [12] She had been brought up in a strictly Puritanical atmosphere and had a particular horror of drink. The father, on the other hand, was quite often drunk and "never went near a chapel." [13] He was a good dancer; knew a great deal about wild life; and, from Ada's description, appears to have been a very handsome man; but he had received very little education and his reading was confined to newspapers. "We used to wonder," wrote Ada, "that mother and father, so utterly unsuitable to each other, should be married." [14] They obviously had the fascination that opposites have for each other, but not enough in common to sustain the original attraction.

Sons and Lovers alone is enough to demonstrate the importance of his father and his mother in Lawrence's life and art. As a child and young man, he obviously sided with his mother against his father. Already in *Sons and Lovers* he is to some extent redressing the balance by presenting his father in a more favorable light, but the mother is still the dominant figure. Later he swung, if anything, toward his father's side, and he conceived a bitter distrust of the *Magna Mater*, the devouring female in the guise of benevolent motherhood. The reaction was excessive, though understandable in relation to Lawrence's own history which comes so near to enacting the classical Oedipus situation.

The influence of his parents should not, however, be thought of primarily in terms of mother-love followed by a compensating idealization of the assertive male, though this must be reckoned an important theme in Lawrence's work. More far-reaching is the principle of duality, linked with the contrasting features of his native region, which it helped to establish in Lawrence's mind. Unlike his sister, Ada—and unlike his earlier self, if Ada's "we" included Lawrence—he came to believe that a man and a woman of such different temperaments as his mother and father were not unsuited to one another, but formed the best foundation for a marriage, though he preferred that the education and control should lie with the man rather than the woman. He was no doubt influenced in this by his own marriage to Frieda Weekley (*née* von Richthofen), a woman of altogether different class and temperament from himself; but it is significant that—when in *The Rainbow* he creates for Tom Brangwen, the Nottinghamshire farmer, a mysteriously foreign wife—he gives her the Christian name of his mother, Lydia.

III *Theory of Duality*

Lawrence's attitude toward the sexes is essentially dualistic. Maleness and femaleness are total for him, and he will not even concede, in his theorizing, that actual men and women share characteristics of the opposite sex. He grants the existence of effeminate men and Amazonian women, but these he regards as perversions of the natural separation of the sexes. In education he is a virulently anti-coeducationist. Male and female are distinct and should be kept so: "A child is either male or female; in the whole of its psyche and physique is either male or female." [15] And, where adults are concerned, Lawrence is even more angrily in disagreement with the "liberal" opinions of enlightened moderns. The creator of Ursula and Gudrun in *The Rainbow* and *Women in Love,* characters who perhaps more than any others in twentieth-century fiction are profound explorations of modern femininity, is among the most conservative of reactionaries when it comes to the question of woman's place in society:

But it is all a fallacy. Man, in the midst of all his effeminacy, is still male and nothing but male. And woman, though she harangue in Parliament or patrol the streets with a helmet on her head, is still completely female. They are only playing each other's roles, because the poles have swung into reversion. The compass is reversed. But that doesn't mean that the north pole has become the south pole, or that each is a bit of both.

Of course a woman should stick to her own natural emotional positivity. But then man must stick to his own positivity of *being,* of action, disinterested, non-domestic, male action, which is not devoted to the increase of the female. Once man vacates his camp of sincere, passionate positivity in disinterested being, his supreme responsibility to fulfil his own profoundest impulses, with reference to none but God or his own soul, not taking woman into count at all, in this primary responsibility to his own deepest soul; once man vacates this strong citadel of his own genuine, not spurious, divinity, then in comes woman, picks up the sceptre and begins to conduct a rag-time band.[16]

The references to "poles" and "positivity" are part of Lawrence's development of his basic notion of duality into an elaborate theory of "polarity." This involves a somewhat odd physiology in which "sympathetic" centers and "voluntary," or assertive, centers exist at higher and lower levels in the human body known as "sensual" and "spiritual" planes. Circuits are set up between these centers, and upon the proper, natural development of the centers and the circuits between them depends the health of the individual psyche. The true goal of education is "the full and harmonious development of the four primary modes of consciousness," [17] not the stimulation of the upper centers associated with "mental consciousness" at the expense of the more animal "sensual" centers.

The ideal informing the theory is that of wholeness of being, which is seen to depend, not on a compromise, or even a wise cooperation between head and heart, but on a dynamic opposition and vivid electric flow of energy between the poles within one human being or "between the individual himself and other individuals concerned in his living; or between him and his immediate surroundings, human, physical, geographical." [18] The disruption of the natural flow, as when a mother tries deliberately to awake in her baby a premature awareness of love and benevolence, leads to a disequilibrium between the four centers which can ultimately be fatal to the human being. Equally, a cold, deliberate use of the will to restrain impulses emanating, for example, from the "sensual" plane can lead to disastrous consequences. (This notion is not unlike that of the Freudian complex, though with obvious differences. Before completing *Sons and Lovers*, Lawrence had become acquainted through Frieda with the outlines of Freudian psychology, which he regarded, however, as "too limited and mechanical." [19])

Over-stimulation of the "spiritual" and denial of the "sensual" were, in fact, for Lawrence the besetting sins of the modern western world. He was a bitter opponent of the Christian ideals of love and benevolence, not out of a sadistic inclination to violence and hate (though it is difficult to resist the conclusion that a sadistic element creeps into works like *The Plumed Serpent* and "The Woman Who Rode Away"), but because he believed them to be limited ideals catastrophically accepted by men as whole and complete—and this despite the fact that human conduct constantly revealed this acceptance as hypocritical. His retelling of the story of Christ's resurrection in "The Escaped Cock"—which may appear sacrilegious to the orthodox Christian—is his most evident attempt to redress what he believed to be the imbalance of Christianity; and the supposed retreat of Christ from Mexico in *The Plumed Serpent* is another.

Lawrence was not, however, irreligious. He described his religion as "a belief in the blood, the flesh, as being wiser than the intellect." [20] This statement, which comes from a letter, should not be taken as a carefully considered expression of Lawrence's religion. It emphasizes what we have already noted in the discussion of his theory of polarity, that "the intellect is only a bit and a bridle" and becomes dangerously tyrannical if allowed to dictate the pattern of man's life. And man's life is only a portion of the forever mysterious vitality of the whole universe with which "the blood, the flesh" is immediately in contact. Sexual intercourse is an important part of Lawrence's belief because it momentarily annihilates mental consciousness (or may do so, if it is not itself mentalized as "sex in the head" [21]) and renews both man and woman by restoring this contact with the extra-human source of life. He has no pornographic fascination with the obscene. On the contrary, he approaches sex with reverence; and he approaches marriage, as a stabilizing of the sexual rhythm between a man and a woman altogether different from the superficial relationship of casual promiscuity, with equal reverence. But for marriage as a social institution, and in general for the principle of the subjection of individuals to the overriding claims of society, he has scant respect.

Even so, Lawrence's individualism is far from being anarchical. It has its origins in the Congregationalism in which he was brought up by his mother; and, although he abandoned the tenets of Protestant Nonconformity (finding Catholicism with its sacramental treatment of the physical more congenial), he retained throughout his life the Nonconformist feeling for the supremacy of the inner light and the voice of conscience. Man should depend neither on reason nor traditional authority (in this respect, he had a profound quarrel with Catholicism), but on obedience to "some deep, inward voice of religious belief. Obeying from within." [22]

IV *Foreign Places*

For Lawrence, World War I was a watershed finally dividing the old England, in which his religion could find nourishment, from the new one dominated by the twin evils of industrialism and tyrannical mental consciousness. As soon as he could obtain a passport, he escaped and spent the rest of his life wandering about Europe, Australia, and America, with only brief return visits to his homeland. His nomadic existence makes him a classic example of the isolation of the modern artist who has become *déraciné*. He was always seeking a new community and a new land where he could put down new roots, but without success. He toyed for a time with the idea of a Utopian experiment in communal living (Rananim), and with more real satisfaction he sought to identify himself with primitive communities which were still relatively unspoilt by industrialism.

His four travel books—*Twilight in Italy, Sea and Sardinia, Mornings in Mexico,* and *Etruscan Places*—are all variations on this theme. In *Twilight in Italy* and in *Sea and Sardinia* Lawrence writes of the Italian peasants who are still capable of a peaceful, creative absorption in the sun and the earth and manual labor. They are like the old spinning woman whose sense that even "the lands she had not seen were corporate parts of her own living body" gave a "wonderful clear unconsciousness to her eyes." [23] Or he writes about the Sardinians who, in their brightly colored peasant costumes, still possess the distinct maleness and femaleness which Lawrence considered so necessary to fine, spontaneous living. But this way of life is already in its "twilight." Many of the Sardinians wear the significantly khaki uniforms of their military service instead of the native costume, and the peasants of the Lake Garda region are infected with the fever of emigration to America.

Lawrence himself is caught between the desire for the past—

I sat on the roof of the lemon-house, with the lake below and the snowy mountain opposite, and looked at the ruins on the old, olive-fuming shores, at all the peace of the ancient world still covered in sunshine, and the past seemed to me so lovely that one must look towards it, backwards, only backwards, where there is peace and beauty and no more dissonances.[24]

—and the feeling that the peasant life, with its "endless heat and rousedness of physical sensation which keeps the body full and potent, and flushes the mind with a blood heat, a blood sleep" at last becomes "a bondage." [25]

It is the same with the experiences recorded in *Mornings in Mexico* and the essays on America in *Phoenix*. On the one hand, there are the recreations of the animistic conceptions of the Indians which reveal Lawrence's profound sympathy with the world of the primitive poetic imagination; on the other, there is an honest recognition of, and instinctive disgust with, the sordid cruelty, "without a touch of tenderness," [26] embodied in the ancient Aztec religion. To the Indians all is alive, whereas "Our cosmos is a great engine. And we die of ennui." [27] But the Indian way of consciousness cannot be connected with ours; nor does Lawrence in the last resort want to surrender his European consciousness:

> Our darkest tissues are twisted in this old tribal experience, our warmest blood came out of the old tribal fire. And they vibrate still in answer, our blood, our tissue. But me, the conscious me, I have gone a long road since then. And as I look back, like memory terrible as bloodshed, the dark faces round the fire in the night, and one blood beating in me and them. But I don't want to go back to them, ah, never. I never want to deny them or break with them. But there is no going back. Always onward, still further. The great devious onward-flowing stream of conscious human blood. From them to me, and from me on. . . . My way is my own, old red father; I can't cluster at the drum any more.[28]

In *Etruscan Places* (along with which one should read *Apocalypse, Last Poems,* and the Preface to *Fantasia of the Unconscious*) Lawrence no longer writes of an actual surviving community but of a pre-Roman world about which comparatively little is known, except what can be inferred from their excavated tombs. This lack of information leaves Lawrence's imagination free to create according to his ideal of the art of living. The passage in Chapter 3, "The Painted Tombs of Tarquinia," describing the Etruscan feeling for life is one of the most moving in Lawrence's work. It recreates what Lawrence believed to have once been a universal "science of life, a conception of the universe and man's place in the universe which made men live to the depth of their capacity." [29] The search is now for a mythical lost Atlantis. Each time Lawrence and his friend Brewster descend into the Etruscan tombs, they enter a marvelous underground world which is not so much an escape from reality as the expression of a creative dissatisfaction with the devitalized world of the surface. Modern Italy and the Italy of its imagined past are counterpointed with poignant effect, and Lawrence himself moves in both worlds.

V *Realism and Romance*

All the travel books are characterized by a blending of realism and romanticism, and in this they are typical of Lawrence's work generally. As Herbert Lindenberger has shown in his essay "Lawrence and the Romantic Tradition," Lawrence's novels combine the traditions of the "novel of social relations" with those of the "symbolist novel" or "romance." [30] And the most important literary influences on his work are those of the English Romantic Movement—with Wordsworth and Blake as the most important individual writers—and of the American offshoots of this movement such as Whitman, Melville, and Fenimore Cooper, on whom Lawrence writes with brilliant critical perceptiveness in *Studies in Classic American Literature*. Other writers whose influence on Lawrence cannot be ignored are Scott, Dickens, George Eliot, Hardy (the novelist who is closest to Lawrence in his writing of the old agricultural England and of whom Lawrence made an unfinished "Study," printed in *Phoenix*), Tolstoi, Dostoevski, Maupassant, and the Italian writer, Giovanni Verga, whose tales, including "Cavalleria Rusticana," Lawrence translated. And, of course, everywhere in Lawrence's work one sees the influence, both in content and style, of the King James Version of the Bible.

A schoolteacher friend says that "He read everything he could lay hands on—plays, verse and novels especially," [31] and Ford Madox Ford writes:

I have never known any young man of his age who was so well read in all the dullnesses that spread between Milton and George Eliot. In himself alone he was the justification of the Education Act . . . he moved amongst the high things of culture with a tranquil assurance that no one trained like myself in the famous middle-class schools of the country ever either exhibited or desired.[32]

The charge of ignorance that is sometimes laid against Lawrence is thus easily refuted. His knowledge, particularly of nineteenth-century literature, was extensive. It was in the nineteenth-century climate of social awareness counterbalanced by glimpses into "unknown modes of being" [33] that his mind was formed, and these two aspects of human experience he strove to integrate in his work. His continuity with previous literature is apparent. But he is also a breaker of new ground, especially in *The Rainbow* and in *Women in Love*. He does not merely consolidate the work of his predecessors; he carries the novel forward into new areas which he explores as he writes and which demand from him a revision of the technique of novel-writing for their expression.

His two principal aims—as stated in his critical essays "Why

the Novel Matters" and "Morality and the Novel"—are to communicate the whole man, "man alive," and to reveal "the chang-
ing rainbow of our living relationships." [34] These involve writing
with a vivid, bristling immediacy that captures the freshness of
sense impressions as they register upon the mind; an honesty and
a faithfulness to the actual quality of human experience which
allow "the trembling instability of the balance" to make itself
felt, together with a refusal by the novelist "to pull down the
balance to his own predilection";[35] and a capacity to understand
and render those implicit laws of life which govern the development of human beings with or without their conscious awareness.
All of these qualities Lawrence's writing has, but not in all places
and at all times.

An unjust comment of T. S. Eliot's is that Lawrence was "a
writer who had to write often badly in order to write sometimes
well." [36] It is certainly true, however, that he often wrote below
his best and that he did not always adhere to his own excellent
principles, especially in the matter of refusing "to pull down the
balance to his own predilection." He possesses both humor and
the capacity for self-criticism, however—qualities which, again,
have often been denied him by his critics; and these frequently
mitigate the effects of his tendencies toward the doctrinaire and
the overearnest. And, though Lawrence may hector and seek to
intimidate his readers, may relapse into vulgarity at times, or may
verge upon the frantically obscure, he does not pontificate or pretend to the false eminence of a literary dictator. It is always a
man who speaks to one from the printed page, never the august
embodiment of literature. As Lawrence wrote to Edward Garnett:

. . . you tell me I am half a Frenchman and one-eighth a Cockney.
But that isn't it. I have very often the vulgarity and disagreeableness
of the common people, as you say Cockney, and I may be a Frenchman. But primarily I am a passionately religious man, and my novels
must be written from the depth of my religious experience. That I must
keep to, because I can only work like that. And my Cockneyism and
commonness are only when the deep feeling doesn't find its way out,
and a sort of jeer comes instead, and sentimentality, and purplism. But
you should see the religious, earnest, suffering man in me first, and
then the flippant or common things after.[37]

CHAPTER 2

The Early Novels:
The White Peacock, The Trespasser,
and Sons and Lovers

LAWRENCE'S early novels, except for *The Trespasser*, are about his native area. He writes about what he knows well, and this is evident in the realism with which he describes people and places, especially in *Sons and Lovers*. But he is not content with this limited aim. His Romantic inheritance makes him also wish to transform the familiar—not to give it a falsely enchanted glamour, but, in Wordsworth's phrase, to throw over it "a certain colouring of imagination, whereby ordinary things should be presented to the mind in an unusual way." [1] The effect can be summarized in this sentence from *The White Peacock*: "I looked down on the blackness where trees filled the quarry, and the valley bottoms, and it seemed that the world, my own home-world, was strange again" (Chap. 11).

Because of Lawrence's experimenting with the combination of realism and romanticism, these early novels form a deeply interesting prelude to his most important novels, *The Rainbow* and *Women in Love*, but they are also of great interest in themselves. Indeed, where *Sons and Lovers* is concerned, it is unjust to allow the two later novels to obscure what is already a very fine achievement. *Sons and Lovers* is an autobiographical work, and this gives it the extraordinary inwardness which is its unique feature; but it is also a remarkable picture of English working-class life and Lawrence's first major study of personal relations.

I   The White Peacock

Lawrence's first novel, *The White Peacock* (written between 1907 and 1909), was described by Ford Madox Ford as "a rotten work of genius," and Lawrence himself was well aware of its faults. In a letter of April 15, 1908, he says:

> In the first place it is a novel of sentiment—may the devil fly away with it—what the critics would call, I believe, an 'erotic novel'—the devil damn the whole race black—, all about love—and rhapsodies on Spring scattered here and there—heroines galore—no plot—nine-tenths adjectives—every colour in the spectrum descanted upon—a poem or two—scraps of Latin and French—altogether a sloppy, spicy mess.

This letter refers to an early version, later revised. The published version is not such "a sloppy, spicy mess," but the weaknesses are still apparent. The "rhapsodies on Spring," and the nature descriptions generally, are lyrical excrescences, often beautiful in themselves and full of an intensely personal feeling for nonhuman life; but they are only loosely related to the novel as a whole.

The "scraps of Latin and French" are mostly used by the educated and socially superior characters. Their effect is pretentious, and this is not altogether accidental. Already *The White Peacock* anticipates, as it does so many other developments in Lawrence's work, the antipathy to "accursed human education" expressed in the poem "Snake." Lettie's deterioration in the latter part of the novel is purposely associated with an increasingly affected and dilettante interest in the arts. The affectation of Cyril, the first-person narrator of the story, is probably equally intentional. (In another letter Lawrence comments that Cyril "is a young fool at the best of times, and a frightful bore at the worst." [2]) Yet there are many self-consciously literary and pretentiously allusive passages in which Cyril is not speaking in his own character, but simply as the narrator, and in these Lawrence's control is not yet firm enough to make one confident that he has detached himself from the affectation which accompanies the narration. If the theme of "accursed human education" forms a serious part of the novel's purpose, it is, one suspects, because the novelist himself is struggling with a tendency which he dislikes, but cannot wholly escape—nor, as yet, see clearly for what it is. As in the poetry which Lawrence writes at this time, there is evidence of a struggle going on between the literary pretensions of a highly self-conscious young man and the "demon" of the true artist.[3]

The two main characters are Lettie and George who have a love affair which is thwarted by class and education. They are not "star-crossed" lovers. Their love is never allowed to develop.

George suffers from a fatal inertia and diffidence that prevent him from seizing the few chances he has with Lettie. He is a farmer's son, from the same yeoman stock as Tom Brangwen in *The Rainbow;* George is physically superb, but sluggish with the heavy earth in which he works. Lettie stirs him as a person who could give meaning and purpose to his life. It is a romantic conception, not of the cheap sort, but lacking in definition. Lawrence, who has too many other interests on hand, cannot explore this relationship and make it urgent and meaningful to the reader.

Lettie's interest in George is ambiguous. His manliness makes a real appeal to her, but the flirt and the snob in her produce a false and dangerous relationship. She uses her refinement as a means of tormenting him and arousing him at the same time. Even after her engagement and marriage to Leslie, son of an important local gentleman mine owner, she cannot resist the temptation to flirt with George. He makes an appeal which is—again, obscurely—deeper than the primarily social appeal of Leslie, and it seems that her denial of this is responsible for the affectation and escape into Motherhood of her subsequent life. George's loss of Lettie has an even more disastrous effect on him. He turns almost self-spitingly to a completely opposite type, Meg, who works at "The Ram," a public house. She has no interest in culture, but is warm and unexactingly vulgar. When the honeymoon glow has worn off, their marriage decays. The children become all-important to Meg, and George finds his refuge in drunkenness. By the end of the novel he is a ruined man.

Lettie and George by no means monopolize the novel. Leslie, Meg, and Cyril, the other characters already mentioned, are also of major importance, and so is Emily. Emily foreshadows Miriam of *Sons and Lovers,* and is, in fact, based on the same girl, Jessie Chambers, who was Lawrence's sweetheart for several years. The list of important minor characters is considerable—Mrs. Beardsall, Mr. and Mrs. Saxton, Alice, Annable (the strange gamekeeper who looks far forward in Lawrence's development to Mellors of *Lady Chatterley's Lover*), and Meg's grandmother. There are yet more who appear in only one or two scenes. *The White Peacock* is a diffuse novel, but, to some extent as a corollary of this, it is also one that has breadth. It takes in a wide range of the Nottinghamshire and Derbyshire countryside, stressing its idyllic charm rather than its industrial ugliness, but certainly not glossing over the latter. And, in the short section that deals with

London, one can see Lawrence trying to include the outcasts who sleep under Waterloo Bridge.

Lying in the novel as a seed, though certainly not yet developed, is the great theme of a Fall. Toward the end of the story Cyril feels his alienation from the small, intimate, and sheltering world of Nethermere: "The valley of Nethermere had cast me out many years before, while I had fondly believed it cherished me in memory." The main characters are cast out from adolescence into unsatisfied adulthood. The horizon broadens from Nethermere to Yorkshire, London, even to Canada where the Saxton family intends to emigrate. Nethermere itself is old and decayed compared with "the tumult of life which had once quickened the valley." It is this poetic suggestiveness which almost, but not quite, gives the novel symbolic status.

The main organizing device is parallelism. The "Father" episode (Chapter 4) forms an anticipatory parallel to the drunken decay of George, and both relate to the Man-Woman, Father-Mother opposition which sharpens as the novel progresses. Through poetic suggestiveness, the otherwise completely extraneous Annable material is related to the rest of the work. Lettie, not in every detail, but in the essential significance of her behavior, repeats the corrupt refinement of Lady Christabel; she is the "white peacock" of the main action. And different as Meg is in personality and education, she has the same urge as Lettie to reduce her man to a servant, if she can. Emily, too, is shown doing this in the final chapter. She is also on the way to becoming a Mother, like Lettie and Meg.

Some of these parallels are crudely handled. Lawrence shows his inexperience in this aspect, as in his handling of the more traditional aspects of the novel. But, despite its rawness and over-adolescent sensibility, *The White Peacock* makes a deep impression. It provides a mirror of English provincial life, and yet suggests that something far more penetrating is at work in the author's mind. From any point of view, it is a remarkable first novel.

II   The Trespasser

The setting of Lawrence's second novel is the Isle of Wight and South London. These derive from his schoolmastering at Croydon and a holiday spent on the Isle of Wight in August, 1909. His friendship with Helen Corke, the Helena of the novel, is, however, the most important source. Helen Corke had undergone a disastrous emotional experience similar to that recorded in *The Trespasser*, of which she gives her own account in her own novel, *Neutral Ground*. Part of the manuscript of this novel formed the basis of *The Trespasser*.

Lawrence began writing his novel in 1910, shortly after Helen Corke's actual experience occurred, but he rewrote it in 1912, feeling distaste for its "fluid, luscious quality," and making an effort at form. ("I hope the thing is knitted firm—I hate those pieces where the stitch is slack and loose." [4]) These comments are very relevant to what the reader feels about the finished novel. There is an element of callowness in the book, by no means dominant, but reflecting perhaps the youthfulness of the earlier draft which Lawrence did not succeed in completely revising away. More positively to the credit of the book is its tightness of structure—the main action takes place within a week; the retrospective frame gives it a certain distance, without detracting from the immediacy of the love idyll; and the overflowing variety of description, incident, and character that is so marked in *The White Peacock* is kept very much more under control. Yet the "fluid, luscious quality" remains an inescapable weakness, and a serious one; for it is as an attempt to render erotic experience that at least half of *The Trespasser* must be judged. Lawrence is making his first real attempt to communicate through poetic prose the powerful, baffling, elusive emotions of sexual experience. He has to cut through the inhibitions imposed in 1912 on any attempt even to imagine seriously what such experience might be, and it is evident in the vagueness of certain passages that Lawrence is not yet so defiant of public taboos as he was to become. His difficulties are greater since he has few, if any, examples to help him in fashioning a technique for suggesting what is largely inarticulate and at the same time integrating it with a theme.

In *The Trespasser* Helena has an affair with a married man, Siegmund, which ends in the latter's suicide. They steal five days on the Isle of Wight away from the sordid complications of Siegmund's wife and children. It is here that the erotic interest of the novel arises. Helena "belonged to that class of 'dreaming women' with whom passion exhausts itself at the mouth." She loves Siegmund, but she cannot respond to his physical passion. The theme is stated fairly baldly toward the end of the Isle of Wight idyll: "Helena had rejected him. She gave herself to her fancies only. For some time she had confused Siegmund with her god. Yesterday she had cried to her ideal lover, and found only Siegmund. It was the spear in the side of his tortured self-respect" (Chap. 19).

Siegmund is fairly well realized as a character, and this fact makes it possible to see that his failure is also due to weakness within himself. He lacks the toughness of mind necessary to suppress qualms and to make unpleasant decisions that must be carried through by strength of will. But the essential blow, given unwittingly by Helena, is the blow to his male self-respect. Their relationship is thus more destructive than creative.

To communicate the ambivalence of their love, Lawrence employs—how deliberately it is impossible to say—devices which are a literary equivalent of the recurrent theme, or leitmotiv, in music. (The method is obviously appropriate, as Siegmund is a violinist, and a constant Wagnerian undertone is kept up by references to *Tristan and Isolde, Lohengrin, Die Walküre,* etc.) The principal recurrent themes are sunshine; natural fertility, especially as suggested by the bee; and death. There are many variations on these, and they are skillfully intertwined.

Siegmund on the island becomes a sunlover. As in the later short story, "Sun," Lawrence links fertility and sunshine as the expression of a physical and spiritual rebirth. Through Helena, Siegmund finds release from the ashy condition into which his life has sunk. In Chapter 8, for example, his own exhilarating sense of vitality affects all the things around him. He bathes and finds the water "as full of life as I am." He feels "a delight in his triumph over the waves." He finds a little bay, inaccessible from the land, which reminds him of Helena; and there are obvious erotic overtones in the account of his finding a sea cave and "creeping into it like a white bee into a white virgin blossom that had waited, how long, for its bee." And then follows an even more intense, and brilliantly effective, passage of indirect erotic description:

The sand was warm to his breast, and his belly, and his arms. It was like a great body he cleaved to. Almost, he fancied, he felt it heaving under him in its breathing. Then he turned his face to the sun, and laughed. All the while, he hugged the warm body of the sea-bay beneath him. He spread his hands upon the sand; he took it in handfuls, and let it run smooth, warm, delightful, through his fingers.

'Surely,' he said to himself, 'it is like Helena'; and he laid his hands again on the warm body of the shore, let them wander, discovering, gathering all the warmth, the softness, the strange wonder of smooth warm pebbles, then shrinking from the deep weight of cold his hand encountered as he burrowed under the surface wrist-deep. In the end he found the cold mystery of the deep sand also thrilling. He pushed in his hands again and deeper, enjoying the almost hurt of the dark, heavy coldness. For the sun and the white flower of the bay were breathing and kissing him dry, were holding him in their warm concave, like a bee in a flower, like himself on the bosom of Helena, and flowing like the warmth of her breath in his hair came the sunshine, breathing near and lovingly; yet, under all, was this deep mass of cold, that the softness and warmth merely floated upon.   (Chap. 8)

Siegmund becomes "a happy priest of the sun"; and, as he approaches Helena who is sitting in a garden "heavy with wild clematis and honeysuckle," there is again the erotic overtone of "a murmur of bees going in and out the brilliant little porches of nasturtium flowers."

The next chapter, which opens with the simple statement, "The day waxed hot," is a brief sun movement. Out of context it might seem merely like a good piece of description, but following on Chapter 8 it is richly evocative. Insistence on the heat takes on the significance of Siegmund's delight in the sun. The phrase, "Siegmund with the sunshine on his forehead," is both literal and metaphorical. "Seed," "seed-dust," "blossoms," "buds," and "budded" form a sequence in the latter half of the chapter which springs naturally out of the heat of the first half. It concludes with the sentence, "He rose somewhat reluctantly from his large fruitful inertia," which is the culmination of the fertility movement initiated by Siegmund's bathing in the previous chapter.

These references to heat and fertility give a special retrospective significance to the very first chapter which had shown Helena several months after Siegmund's death. Her arm, strangely enough, still flamed with the sunburn which she caught on her Isle of Wight holiday, and she had described herself as a tree unable to shed its dead leaves. The suggestion is that this is far more than a metaphor for her inability to forget Siegmund and let herself be wooed by a new lover. The sunshine is an experience so powerful as to be dangerous. This is hinted at in Siegmund as well. He exposes himself willfully to the sun. "I like the sunshine on me," he claims, "real, and manifest, and tangible. I feel like a seed that has been frozen for ages. I want to be bitten by the sunshine." "Bitten" is here no slip of the pen, creating an unwanted discordance. Its harshness is reflected in the painfulness that comes from exposure to the sun. As the end of the brief holiday draws near, Siegmund lies on the beach, his forehead "swollen and inflamed with the sun" and his eyes so dazzled by it that he cannot see. The night before his suicide, this heat turns into a fever which is clearly part of an attack of sunstroke. Finally, on "a hot, still morning, when everything outdoors shone brightly, and all indoors was dusked with coolness and colour" Siegmund hangs himself.

The presence of death in love is a traditionally romantic theme, and *The Trespasser* is to some extent a work of romance. (Lawrence gives ample hint of a parallel with the story of Tristan and Isolde.) But, as the second half of the novel makes strikingly apparent, the writer of the scenes at "The Ram" in *The White Peacock* is also evident in *The Trespasser*. In the train that takes the two lovers back to London, Siegmund begins to reckon the complications of his adultery; and, from the moment he reaches his home, the atmosphere is completely changed. The novel becomes a bitterly realistic treatment of the misery of a defecting husband, the coldly self-righteous anger of an injured wife, and the repercussions of their behavior upon the children.

The shock caused by this change in the novel must not be underestimated. Lawrence no doubt knew what he was doing. Intensely romantic a writer as he was, he was also, even in his very earliest work, not only a realist but also a sardonic antiromantic. He pitches his readers almost brutally from the idyllic world of the Isle of Wight into the grating realism of Siegmund's domestic life. This transfer does not, however, toughen the story in quite the way that Lawrence intended. Instead, it seals off the island experience as a cruelly temporary escape from reality. The imaginative devices that have already been discussed provide a connection between the two halves of the book, but not one that is strong enough to overcome the shock of the sudden and complete transition that takes place in Chapter 22. The extremely difficult problem of welding together romanticism and realism is left unsolved.

III   Sons and Lovers

Sons and Lovers begins with a fine historical and geographical sweep of the Nottinghamshire and Derbyshire coal field. The beginning also contains within it the criticism of industrialism which Lawrence was to develop so much more fully later. The original small mines "scarcely soiled" the brook that ran by Hell Row. Power was provided by donkeys. They were ancient mines, and men and animals and the mines themselves formed a continuous part of the life of nature: "And all over the countryside were these same pits, some of which had been worked in the time of Charles II, the few colliers and the donkeys burrowing down like ants into the earth, making queer mounds and little black places among the corn-fields and the meadows" (Chap. 1).

Then—Lawrence's verb makes its own comment—"The gin-pits were elbowed aside by the large mines of the financiers." Railways and new pit-heads spread over the countryside, forming "black studs . . . linked by a loop of fine chain." In place of the cottages which formerly went "straying over the parish" of Bestwood, the Company built "great quadrangles of dwellings" to accommodate what are now called "the regiments of miners."

It would, however, be an oversimplification to say that these opening paragraphs give a merely negative account of the destruction which accompanies the advent of full-scale industrialism. Hell Row deserved its name, and, when it was burned down, "much dirt was cleansed away." And at least one of the new mines—the very one, in fact, where Mr. Morel works—is described as "a large mine among corn-fields." As Lawrence brings his focus on to the particular, one sees, too, that the new houses are "substantial and very decent." Their front gardens are neat and full of flowers. They give rise to squalid conditions of living only because the colliers' wives will not use their front parlors, preferring to make the kitchen the center of domestic life—and the kitchens open on to a "nasty alley of ash-pits." Nature and industrialism thus continue to be sharply juxtaposed, but there is not quite the same irreconcilable opposition as in "Nottingham and the Mining Countryside."

The toughness of mind and the strength of will that are the driving force of industry are given less hostile treatment in *Sons and Lovers* than in the rest of Lawrence's novels. Mrs. Morel above all has these qualities; they are evident not only in her painfully prolonged resistance to death, but also in her heroic determination to resist the spiritually deadening effect of life in a mining community. Her unconscious tyranny over her sons, the primary theme of the novel and what makes it a tragedy, is perhaps to be connected with the evil influence of industrialism; but the grit which her life develops in her, and which she hands on to her son Paul, is also part of working-class life as Lawrence displays it in the Morel home. Dorothy van Ghent cites the passage in which Paul speaks of the pit as being "like something alive—a big creature that you don't know," and she claims that in *Sons and Lovers* work in the colliery "is still symbolic of the greater rhythm governing life and obedience to which is salvation." [5] This is probably overweighting a detail (though it is interestingly like the moment in *The Trespasser* when Siegmund's feeling for city movement is contrasted with Helen's wish always to escape to the country), but it does contribute to the impression, springing from the whole novel, that industrialism is not merely grindingly destructive, but the product of a potentially strong, creative source.

Lawrence said that *Sons and Lovers* would be "a novel—not a florid prose poem, or a decorated idyll running to seed in realism." [6] In other words, it would avoid the faults of both *The White Peacock* and *The Trespasser*. One way in which it does this is by being solidly embedded in the working-class life that Lawrence thoroughly understood. He does not attempt this time to transpose his relatives and friends into a higher social class. They are as they were in real life. The result is an exceptionally vivid portrayal of the ordinary surface of working-class life in the English Midlands as it was near the beginning of the twentieth century. The first part of the novel breaks out again and again into little dramatically alert scenes of common life that remain in the memory as captured glimpses of an intense and intimate domestic existence highly charged with passionate feelings which those who share them could not normally articulate. This is the great difference between working-class and middle-class life. There are subtleties of relationship, though nothing like the subtleties of a cultured middle-class world; and there are unconscious pressures toward conformity that are possibly even stronger than those of the middle class. At the same time there is a large, crude mold into which all life is forced.

The Morel family is an exceptional family, it must be granted, as, quite obviously the actual Lawrence family was; but it is still a true working-class family—for working-class life is not all a brutal "I'm all right, Jack," *Saturday Night and Sunday Morning* affair. What Alan Sillitoe presents is true to a part of that life, but, generally speaking, it is the part that the working people themselves regard as belonging to the slums. And most working people resent identification with it. Lawrence's Morel family embodies the aspirations of the working class—some of them pathetic enough, such as the belief in the superiority of a white-collar, commercial job; but their ambitions give a purpose to life which puts it far beyond the mere work-eat-drink level of existence.

In any case, Mr. Morel is not exceptional in the same way. He does not fret against the crude mold as his wife does, but seems reasonably content with conditions as he finds them. The conflict between himself and his wife is therefore a conflict between two elements in the working-class way of life. It is, of course, also very much a conflict of personality. Lawrence summarizes this aspect in the well-known passage contrasting Mr. and Mrs. Morel:

> Walter Morel seemed melted away before her. She was to the miner that thing of mystery and fascination, a lady. When she spoke to him, it was with a southern pronunciation and a purity of English which thrilled him to hear. She watched him. He danced well, as if it were natural and joyous in him to dance. . . . a certain subtle exultation like glamour in his movement, and his face the flower of his body, ruddy, with tumbled black hair, and laughing alike whatever partner he bowed above. She thought him rather wonderful, never having met anyone like him. . . . Gertrude herself was rather contemptuous of dancing; she had not the slightest inclination towards that accomplishment, and had never learned even a Roger de Coverley. She was a puritan, like her father, high-minded, and really stern. Therefore the dusky, golden softness of this man's sensuous flame of life, that flowed off his flesh like the flame from a candle, not baffled and gripped into incandescence by thought and spirit as her life was, seemed to her something wonderful, beyond her. (Chap. 1)

This attraction soon turns into repulsion, but a certain bond remains between husband and wife for a long time. The unlikeness of their characters and upbringing inevitably causes friction which is all the more intense because it coincides with the friction inherent in the tensions of working-class life. To this extent the Mr. and Mrs. Morel of *Sons and Lovers* embody both a psychological and a social study of working-class conflict.

Many episodes in the novel could be used to illustrate this friction, but one is particularly apposite. This is the scene in which Mr. Morel cuts the curls off baby William's head. This comes at the first stage of disillusionment in the marriage of the couple: "At last Mrs. Morel despised her husband. She turned from the father. . . . There began a battle between the husband and wife." In this conflict Mrs. Morel uses her sharpness of tongue, and Mr. Morel retaliates by deliberately exaggerating his coarseness and brutality. Then comes the hair-cutting episode:

> William was only one year old, and his mother was proud of him, he was so pretty. She was not well off now, but her sisters kept the boy in clothes. Then, with his little white hat curled with an ostrich feather, and his white coat, he was a joy to her, the twining wisps of air clustering round his head. Mrs. Morel lay listening, one Sunday morning, to the chatter of the father and child downstairs. Then she dozed off. When she came downstairs, a great fire glowed in the grate, the room was hot, the breakfast was roughly laid, and seated in his armchair against the chimney-piece, sat Morel, rather timid; and standing between his legs, the child—cropped like a sheep, with such an odd round poll—looking wondering at her; and on a newspaper spread out upon the hearthrug, a myriad of crescent-shaped curls, like the petals of a marigold scattered in the reddening firelight.
>
> Mrs. Morel stood still. It was her first baby. She went very white, and was unable to speak.
>
> 'What dost think o' 'im?' Morel laughed uneasily.
>
> She gripped her two fists, lifted them, and came forward. Morel shrank back.
>
> 'I could kill you, I could!' she said. She choked with rage, her two fists uplifted.
>
> 'Yer non want ter make a wench on 'im,' Morel said, in a frightened tone, bending his head to shield his eyes from hers. His attempt at laughter had vanished.
>
> The mother looked down at the jagged, close-clipped head of her child. She put her hands on his hair, and stroked and fondled his head.
>
> 'Oh—my boy!' she faltered. Her lips trembled, her face broke, and, snatching up the child, she buried her face in his shoulder and cried painfully. She was one of those women who cannot cry; whom it hurts as it hurts a man. It was like ripping something out of her, her sobbing. (Chap. 1)

The prettiness of the boy is obviously a protest against, and a form of escape from, the disappointments that Mrs. Morel has suffered. His white coat, white hat with ostrich feather, and particularly his "twining wisps of hair" are in sharp contrast to the blackness of the colliers and the ash heaps of the Bottoms. By cutting off these curls, Mr. Morel injures both his wife's love for the child and her social aspirations. The intensity of her reaction is measured by the language she uses. Instead of making the kind of satirically loaded remark that she applies to Morel when he comes home drunk, she flashes out with, "I could kill you, I could!" and then bursts into sobbing. The qualification, "She was one of those women who cannot cry. . . ." is very important, too. It emphasizes the unusualness of such a response from her, and so displays the strength of her feeling on this occasion.

Lawrence goes on to say, after the passage quoted above, that Mrs. Morel admitted the need for the child's hair to be cut sooner or later: "In the end, she even brought herself to say to her husband it was just as well he had played barber when he did." Her natural grit and her common sense enable her to deal with the situation, to appear at least to dismiss it as a trivial irritation. She returns to her superficially unromantic self. From the rest of the novel there is certainly no reason to suppose that the white coat, the ostrich feather, and the curly hair have any habitual attractions for Mrs. Morel. Her puritanism works rather against prettiness and charm. (When her grown-up eldest son, William, brings home his befrilled fiancée, the mother's disapproval is obvious enough.)

But the aspirations for which the curls are temporarily a symbol are of a much more serious nature, and it is these which have been outraged. For this reason Lawrence's final comment on the scene—"that act had caused something momentous to take place in her soul. She remembered the scene all her life, as one in which she had suffered the most intensely"—is not a melodramatic exaggeration. It points to the basic conflict which underlies the episode, without defining it explicitly since that would destroy its peculiar quality of realism. The actors do not know exactly what it is that they are acting out, and Lawrence's faithfulness to this aspect of the experience gives the scene not only a greater immediacy of impact but also a much greater working-class veracity.

Apart from its importance as a working-class novel *Sons and Lovers*, as its title suggests, is a great novel about mother love and its relationship to sexual love. The indispensable piece of explication in this respect is Lawrence's letter to Edward Garnett of November 14, 1912, in which he outlines the novel's "idea":

. . . a woman of character and refinement goes into the lower class, and has no satisfaction in her own life. She has had a passion for her husband, so the children are born of passion, and have heaps of vitality. But as her sons grow up she selects them as lovers—first the eldest, then the second. These sons are *urged* into life by their reciprocal love of their mother—urged on and on. But when they come to manhood, they can't love, because their mother is the strongest power in their lives, and holds them. It's rather like Goethe and his mother and Frau von Stein and Christiana— As soon as the young men come into contact with women, there's a split. William gives his sex to a fribble, and his mother holds his soul. But the split kills him, because he doesn't know where he is. The next son gets a woman who fights for his soul —fights his mother. The son loves the mother—all the sons hate and are jealous of the father. The battle goes on between the mother and the girl, with the son as object. The mother gradually proves stronger, because of the tie of blood. The son decides to leave his soul in his mother's hands, and, like his elder brother, go for passion. He gets passion. Then the split begins to tell again. But, almost unconsciously, the mother realises what is the matter, and begins to die. The son casts off his mistress, attends to his mother dying. He is left in the end naked of everything, with the drift towards death.

But as various critics have said, the novel is somewhat different. The "idea" as thus set out by Lawrence implies a degree of detachment from the mother-figure which is not wholly, or at least, not consistently, realized in *Sons and Lovers*. No doubt this has a great deal to do with the fact that the work is fictionalized autobiography, and with the fact, pointed out by Graham Hough, that Lawrence has a tendency to hammer out an interpretation of his own experience in his fiction. The immediacy and fluidly vital quality of Lawrence's work, which give his readers the peculiarly exciting sense of living through an experience with gradually unfolding understanding, derive from this method of writing. But it can also have the result that the material upon which the artist works may remain in some places recalcitrant to the theme which eventually emerges from the work as a whole. Translated into these terms, the "idea" which Lawrence communicated to Edward Garnett is the main theme, but the vivid, local life of the novel sometimes appears inconsistent with it.

To be quite blunt about it, Mrs. Morel is given oversympathetic treatment. The intense love that Lawrence felt for his own mother is probably responsible for a disequilibrium in a presentation of Paul's mother and father which is harmful to the main theme. ". . . all the sons hate and are jealous of the father"—this involves presenting the father unattractively, but if the sons are to be seen as victims of the mother-love, the father must also have an independent existence strong enough for him to be at least potentially attractive to the reader. It is interesting to note how in the later "Nottingham and the Mining Countryside" Lawrence works hard to give his father an independent status. But in *Sons and Lovers* the scenes in which the father is attractively presented are those in which he is either temporarily reconciled to his wife or engaged in practical tasks about the house which virtually concede the woman's superiority. And too often the reader is invited to share in the conspiracy of mother and children against the husband. All the great scenes of warm, subtly responsive intimacy—the scenes in which familiar details of ordinary life are raised to an imaginative level, so that one might without flippancy call Lawrence the Wordsworth of the novel—are shared between Mrs. Morel and her children, especially Paul. An example is the return of Mrs. Morel from Bestwood market:

> She dropped her string bag and her packages on the table.
> 'Is the bread done?' she asked, going to the oven.
> 'The last one is soaking,' he replied. 'You needn't look. I've not forgotten it.'
> 'Oh, that pot man!' she said, closing the oven door. 'You know what a wretch I've said he was? Well, I don't think he's quite so bad.'
> 'Don't you?'
> The boy was attentive to her. She took off her little black bonnet.
> 'No. I think he can't make any money—well, it's everybody's cry alike nowadays—and it makes him disagreeable.'
> 'It would *me*,' said Paul.
> 'Well, one can't wonder at it. And he let me have—how much do you think he let me have *this* for?'
> She took the dish out of its rag of newspaper, and stood looking on it with joy.
> 'Show me!' said Paul.
> The two stood together gloating over the dish.
> 'I *love* cornflowers on things,' said Paul.
> 'Yes, and I thought of the teapot you bought me—'
> 'One and three,' said Paul.
> 'Fivepence!'
> 'It's not enough, mother.'
> 'No. Do you know, I fairly sneaked off with it. But I'd been extravagant, I couldn't afford any more. And he needn't have let me have it if he hadn't wanted to.'
> 'No, he needn't, need he,' said Paul, and the two comforted each other from the fear of having robbed the pot man.
> 'We c'n have stewed fruit in it,' said Paul.

'Or custard, or a jelly,' said his mother.
'Or radishes and lettuce,' said he.
'Don't forget that bread,' she said, her voice bright with glee.
Paul looked in the oven; tapped the loaf on the base.
'It's done,' he said, giving it to her.
She tapped it also.   (Chap. 4)

Mother and son are here loving conspirators in their admiration of the pot and in their mutual concern at having "robbed" the potman. Paul plays up naturally to his mother ("It would *me*") by overestimating the price to intensify the delicious thrill of finding that it was as low as fivepence and by suggesting uses for the pot. And this part of the scene is effectively framed by the business of the bread, a shared activity. Paul taps the loaf. Mrs. Morel taps it also, not because she doesn't trust his judgment, but because it is as much a shared experience as the appreciation of her purchases.

The husband is excluded from such intimacy as this. In fact, it is a particularly happy time for the family when injury keeps him in the hospital incapable of becoming a drunken intruder. Lawrence does suggest occasionally that this is a deplorable slight upon the man, but the sense of delightful intimacy when the father is out of the way and when Paul can proclaim, "I'm the man in the house now," is too strong for these twinges of remorse to prevail.

The same weighting of evidence in favor of the mother is apparent in the second part of the novel when the love affair of Paul and Miriam becomes the most important subject. Baking of bread provides another significant scene here. It is by no means a straightforward one. Miriam comes to visit Paul when he is alone one evening, left in charge of the bread which is finishing baking. A friend, Beatrice, interrupts them and proceeds to tease Miriam and to flirt with Paul. It is Beatrice who actually causes Paul to forget the bread until it is burned. Knowing that his mother will be upset, he is upset too, and tries to hide the evidence. Miriam cannot understand the fuss he is making—"what is it, after all—twopence ha'penny." Paul replies, "Yes, but—it's the mater's precious baking, and she'll take it to heart." The earlier scene is essential to the reader's understanding why. When Mrs. Morel returns she discovers the burning. Paul comes in late from seeing Miriam home, and there is a row which begins with Paul's admitting that he forgot the bread, adding the angry comment, "it's only two-

pence ha'penny. I can pay you for that." Mrs. Morel does not, of
course, know that this was Miriam's comment, but the reader
does; and it has the curious effect of heightening a prejudice
against Miriam—for having, as it were, a bad influence on Paul,
and for debasing the intimacy, which she cannot be expected to
understand or share, in which breadmaking involves mother and
son. The row proceeds to actual condemnation of Miriam, with
Paul as her nominal defender:

'I should have thought,' said Mrs. Morel bitterly, 'that she wouldn't
have occupied you so entirely as to burn a whole ovenful of bread.'
'Beatrice was here as well as she.'
'Very likely. But we know why the bread is spoilt.'
'Why?' he flashed.
'Because you were engrossed with Miriam,' replied Mrs. Morel hotly.
'Oh, very well—then it was *not!*' he replied angrily.   (Chap. 8)

Already the defense has ruined Miriam's case.
The trivial incident is, of course, made electric by the mother's
jealousy. The row proceeds to the stage where Mrs. Morel offers
herself as sharer of Paul's intellectual interests in place of Miriam
—"'How do you know I don't care? Do you ever try me?'"—
and finally to a virtual confession from Mrs. Morel that she is
seeking Paul as a substitute for her husband:

'I can't bear it. I could let another woman—but not her. She'd leave
me no room, not a bit of room—'
And immediately he hated Miriam bitterly.
'And I've never—you know, Paul—I've never had a husband—not
really—'
He stroked his mother's hair, and his mouth was on her throat.
'And she exults so in taking you from me—she's not like ordinary
girls.'
'Well, I don't love her, mother,' he murmured, bowing his head and
hiding his eyes on her shoulder in misery. His mother kissed him a
long, fervent kiss.   (Chap. 8)

According to the "idea" of *Sons and Lovers*, this is a vicious climax; it should be deplorable to see Miriam misrepresented and
abused; but this is not the effect. Hatred of Miriam which springs
in Paul as his mother makes her deep appeal to him is completely
condoned. The effect is not even that of amoral pathos. The emo-

tions generated within the scene swing sympathy positively to the mother's side.

This is not to say that Lawrence is actually *forgetting* his "idea." There is a brilliant bit of satire following immediately on this scene which is intended to "place" it, and would do if the mother-feelings had not gathered such strength. Morel in a drunken condition interrupts the embrace of mother and son:

'At your mischief again?' he said venomously.
Mrs. Morel's emotion turned into sudden hate of the drunkard who had come in thus upon her.
'At any rate, it is sober,' she said.
'H'm—h'm! H'm—h'm!' he sneered.   (Chap. 8)

In view of the importance of drunkenness in this novel—as in *The White Peacock* and in the short story "Odour of Chrysanthemums"—this is a daring balancing of two kinds of drunkenness which ought powerfully to reinforce the central theme of the novel. And it does make its point, but without the full forcefulness that it should have.

With this large qualification about the weight given to the mother's point of view, *Sons and Lovers* does conform to the pattern outlined in the letter to Edward Garnett. The first part of the novel shows that the origin of the split which is to afflict the sons is in the incompatibility of the parents and in the marital frustration resulting from this. In the second part Paul is seen involved with two women—Clara and Miriam—who in many ways correspond to his parents. Miriam is so much resented by Mrs. Morel because she is a competitor for her son's love on the same ground as herself. Both exercise a motherly possessiveness over Paul. Mrs. Morel has a dislike of sentiment which makes her despise Miriam's soulfulness, and she strongly influences her son in feeling the same way about his sweetheart; but it is significant that both women are puritanical by nature. Miriam's interest in Paul's art is more genuine than Mrs. Morel's. The remark, "It was not his art Mrs. Morel cared about; it was himself and his achievement," suggests that she appreciates his painting as the means of his "getting on." Miriam appreciates it for its own sake. But she has an irritating way of assuming a kind of right over everything that Paul produces. They are both unwilling, or unable, to let Paul stand on his own feet. Mrs. Morel says of Miriam: "She is one of those who will want to suck a man's soul out till he has none of his own left . . . and he is just such a gaby as to let himself be absorbed. She will never let him become a man; she never will" (Chap. 7). The irony of the remark is that it is even more disastrously applicable to the mother herself.

Paul's second sweetheart, Clara, has the sensuous quality of Mr. Morel. Paul's awareness of "the blonde hair" which "grew low and fluffy" on her neck and the "fine down, almost invisible, upon the skin of her face and arms" recalls Mrs. Morel's sensuous awareness of the man who was to become her husband. Clara's attachment to the suffragette movement seems to be included mainly to emphasize her alienation from intellectual life. There is obvious point in her recognition of the nature of Miss Limb's slightly crazed love for her stallion: "'I suppose,' blurted Clara suddenly, 'she wants a man'." Clara herself belongs to the instinctive, untrammeled passionate world of the stallion. The first lovemaking between her and Paul is accompanied by the flood-swollen River Trent, "travelling in a soft body," "the full, soft-sliding Trent," and the carnations which Paul has bought for her are crushed "like splashed drops of blood." Through her he reaches the basic, impersonal life of nature. She seems to have "a certain heaviness, the heaviness of a very full ear of corn that dips slightly in the wind"; and, when their lovemaking is at its finest, it becomes a religious experience of a pantheistic kind:

And after such an evening they both were very still, having known the immensity of passion. They felt small, half afraid, childish, and wondering, like Adam and Eve when they lost their innocence and realized the magnificence of the power which drove them out of Paradise and across the great night and the great day of humanity. It was for each of them an initiation and a satisfaction. To know their own nothingness, to know the tremendous living flood which carried them always, gave them rest within themselves. If so great a magnificent power could overwhelm them, identify them altogether with itself, so that they knew they were only grains in the tremendous heave that lifted every grass-blade its little height, and every tree, and living thing, then why fret about themselves? They could let themselves be carried by life, and they felt a sort of peace each in the other. (Chap. 13)

According to Lawrence himself, the mother "almost unconsciously" realizes how she is preventing her son from achieving his own independence, "and begins to die." The "almost unconsciously" makes it difficult to quarrel with this statement. Lawrence does manage to suggest that Mrs. Morel at last realizes that it is better for Paul to marry even Miriam than to carry on in his restless, drifting fashion. There is no suggestion, however, that her death is a kind of resignation on her part. She clings to life tenaciously; and, when the parson comforts her that she will have her mother and father and sisters and her son "in the Other Land," she replies: "It is the living I want, not the dead."

Paul is the one who wants her to die. Her suffering is too painful for him. He discourages her from taking nourishing food, and in the end he commits what is virtually an act of euthanasia by giving her an overdose of morphine. It is more plausible to regard this act as at last an assertion of independence "almost unconsciously" by Paul. Some minor support is given to this suggestion by the fact that the earlier signs of Mrs. Morel's illness coincide with the beginnings of his resistance to her will over Miriam. (The burning of the bread discussed above is complicated by one of these premonitory attacks.) And after her death, although Paul is "derelict," and there is on almost the last page of the novel a moving paragraph evoking Paul's sense of annihilation, there is still a tiny amount of grit of determination, inherited from his mother at her earlier best, that will not let him give in. The novel actually concludes with:

'Mother!' he whispered—'mother!'
She was the only thing that held him up, himself, amid all this. And she was gone, intermingled herself. He wanted her to touch him, have him alongside with her.
But no, he would not give in. Turning sharply, he walked towards the city's gold phosphorescence. His fists were shut, his mouth set fast. He would not take that direction, to the darkness, to follow her. He walked towards the faintly humming, glowing town, quickly.

This ends *Sons and Lovers* where it had begun, with the individual in relation to the industrial society, here embodied in the city of Nottingham, in which Paul's life has to be lived out. The back-to-the-womb temptation, merging with the romantic death wish which lurks in the pages of *The Trespasser*, is resisted by Paul-Lawrence. And this is only one aspect, though naturally the most striking, of the general refusal in *Sons and Lovers* to retreat from tough realities into attitudes of romantic escape. As already indicated, this is a great novel of naturalistically presented working-class life, "probably the only one written completely from the inside." [7] The sordid and brutal features are accepted as well as the "life itself, warmth" that Paul claims is the heritage of "the common people."

Yet romance penetrates to the humblest details of this life—as in the Wordsworthian quality of the pot scene. In *The Trespasser* realism and romance had split the novel into two parts, but in *Sons and Lovers* they come much nearer to coalescing. At the very least, the novel moves between the two easily, without a jolting change of gear. For example, after the row which concludes with Morel shutting his wife out of the house, Mrs. Morel wanders into the front garden. She becomes aware that "the tall white lilies were reeling in the moonlight, and the air was charged with their perfume, as with a presence." The scent "almost made her dizzy." This hypnotic experience is very different in quality from the row which preceded it, but the fact that Mrs. Morel is pregnant, and that the row has passionately aroused her, contributes, of course, to its effectiveness. It is embedded in the familiar. It carries over, too, into the familiar, for when Mrs. Morel finally gets to bed she smiles faintly "to see her face all smeared with the yellow dust of lilies."

Certain of the more exotic experiences which are thus imbedded in common life have a symbolic function. When Mrs. Morel takes the baby Paul out for a walk on a late summer evening, Lawrence's descriptive prose evokes a sense of plenitude and calm, associated with the sheaves and haystacks of harvest time. Against this background, Mrs. Morel has a feeling of heaviness about her child, "almost as if it were unhealthy, or malformed," and as her emotion grows stronger—complicated by her remembering that she had not wanted the child because of the broken relationship between herself and her husband, and by the desire which she now has to "make up to it for having brought it into the world unloved"—she has a sudden impulse to hold the child up to the sun to which it had earlier been groping: "She thrust the infant forward to the crimson, throbbing sun, almost with relief. She saw him lift his little fist. Then she put him to her bosom again, ashamed of her impulse to give him back again whence he came" (Chap. 2).

Soon she goes home, and "A fine shadow was flung over the

deep green meadow, darkening all." This imaginatively summarizes the theme of the novel, and, coming near the beginning of the novel, it has something of a prophetic import. It hints at Mrs. Morel's refusal to allow Paul to develop his own independent connection with the great, impersonal source of life. As symbolism it is frail compared with certain of the great passages in *The Rainbow* and in *Women in Love,* but it marks an important step forward from the rather stuck-on symbolism of *The White Peacock.* Its integration with the rest of the novel is real and convincing.

Finally, the romantic element in *Sons and Lovers* has an intricate relationship with character, especially the character of Miriam. An extremely sensitive girl, she has been reduced by her mother's mistaken high-mindedness to a semineurotic condition; and, as the love affair between her and Paul develops, her terror of sex becomes a serious barrier between them (though one might also add that Paul's clumsiness and selfishness create an even greater block). There were, perhaps, didactic implications here for Lawrence about the rights of the body as against the spirit. The sardonic remark that it could not be mentioned between them "that the mare was in foal" is one example of this. But the important thing for the novel is the faithfulness with which Lawrence renders the quality of sensibility which this produces in Miriam. "There was no looseness or abandon about her. Everything was gripped stiff with intensity, and her effort, overcharged, closed in on itself." When Paul teaches her algebra and grows angry because, in his statement of the case, she tries to learn it with her soul instead of her wits, the reader is made aware of a much more complicated psychological state of affairs. The frustrations in Miriam are hidden from her lover and from herself, but they are communicated through the evocative power of the prose.

Miriam's taste in poetry is significant:

> . . . She did not like Baudelaire, on the whole—or Verlaine.
> *'Behold her singing in the field*
> *Yon solitary highland lass.'*
> That nourished her heart. So did 'Fair Ines'. And—
> *'It is a beauteous evening, calm and free,*
> *The holy time is quiet as a nun.'*
> These were like herself. (Chap. 8)

Perhaps most of all, the peculiar way in which she responds to flowers communicates the quality of her romantic sensibility. This for example, is how she treats the daffodils at Willey Farm:

> Miriam went on her knees before one cluster, took a wild-looking daffodil between her hands, turned up its face of gold to her, and bowed down, caressing it with her mouth and cheeks and brow. He [Paul] stood aside, with his hands in his pockets, watching her. One after another she turned up to him the faces of the yellow, bursten flowers appealingly, fondling them lavishly all the while.
>
> 'Aren't they magnificent?' she murmured.
>
> 'Magnificent! it's a bit thick—they're pretty!'   (Chap. 9)

Paul's rough answer emphasizes the author's detachment from this religious attitude. Though, as he is forced, often reluctantly, to admit, Miriam's sensibility stimulates him into brilliant conscious activity, he rejects her disembodied religious ecstasy in favor of a plainer, grittier determination. When on holiday by the Lincolnshire coast, he rationalizes this into the difference between the Norman and the Gothic:

> . . . they, the great levels of sky and land in Lincolnshire, meant to him the eternality of the will, just as the bowed Norman arches of the church, repeating themselves, meant the dogged leaping forward of the persistent human soul, on and on, nobody knows where; in contradiction to the perpendicular lines and to the Gothic arch, which, he said, leapt up at heaven and touched the ecstasy and lost itself in the divine. Himself, he said, was Norman, Miriam was Gothic.   (Chap. 7)

It is clear how this difference of sensibility, and criticism of Miriam's sensibility, connects with the struggle in personal relations which is the major theme of the novel. Not only is Miriam defeated by Paul's mother, but she is to some extent crippled by her own romanticism. Like Helen's fancifulness in *The Tres-passer,* this romanticism is something which is at odds with commonplace reality. Paul, and Lawrence through him, by no means rejects the romantic, but he needs to disentangle himself from Miriam's kind. The novel as a whole shows how a more vital romanticism is being developed, and one of the fine effects of the work is the balancing and contrasting of these two kinds. But there is no mere advocacy of the one and rejection of the other. They both form an integral part of the novel as a rich and complex reflection of life. Even the unreal is real in such a setting, for it is part of vital human experience. The finest achievement of *Sons and Lovers* is this quickening truthfulness to actual life—"the shimmering protoplasm" which Paul tries to capture in his paintings, and which is "the real living." Without the romantic element it would simply be, to quote Paul again, "a dead crust."

CHAPTER 3

The Rainbow

I *Genesis and Form*

LAWRENCE took a lot of trouble over *The Rainbow*. He wrote it in 1913-14, in several drafts, and it was published in September, 1915, only to be suppressed on November 13. He felt strongly that it was something new, and the letters which refer to it are of exceptional critical interest. The earliest reference is in a letter of March 11, 1913, to Edward Garnett:

I am a damned curse unto myself. I've written rather more than half of a most fascinating (to me) novel. But nobody will ever dare to publish it. I feel I could knock my head against the wall. Yet I love and adore this new book. It's all crude as yet, like one of Tony's clumsy prehistorical beasts—most cumbersome and floundering—but I think it's great—so new, so really a stratum deeper than I think anybody has ever gone, in a novel. But there, you see, it's my latest. It is all analytical—quite unlike *Sons and Lovers*, not a bit visualised.

Writing to Garnett in April, he states it is "a queer novel, which seems to have come by itself," and "it hasn't got hard outlines." The subject matter as well as the method is of great importance to Lawrence: "I can only write what I feel pretty strongly about: and that, at present, is the relation between men and women. After all, it is *the* problem of today, the establishment of a new relation, or the readjustment of the old one, between men and women." A further reference in a letter of May–June, 1913, seems to be in response to some criticism of Garnett's: "All along I knew what ailed the book. But it did me good to theorise myself out, and to depict Frieda's God Almightiness in all its glory. That was the first crude fermenting of the book. I'll make it into art now."

Possibly at this stage the new thing that Lawrence was working out was coming in too doctrinal a form. The vestiges of this remain in the finished version. The reference to Frieda suggests that the book is an attempt to grapple with the most important experience to come into Lawrence's life in these years: his meeting and elopement with Frieda Weekley (*née* von Richthofen). Her influence is detectable in *Sons and Lovers* and probably in *The Trespasser*, but it is in *The Rainbow* that the upheaval she caused in Lawrence begins to have a radical effect. He refers on January 29, 1914, to making the mistake in his characterization of Ella (later to become Ursula) "of trying to graft on to the character of Louie, the character, more or less, of Frieda"; but as the poems in *Look! We Have Come Through!* suggest, the influence was much more than the providing of a new, and disconcertingly different, model for a character. Frieda gave him a completely new conception of the vital, independent woman and of the life-and-death battle of the sexes.

A letter at the very end of 1913 again refers to the great difference in manner between *The Rainbow* and *Sons and Lovers:* "It is *very* different from *Sons and Lovers:* written in another language almost. I shall be sorry if you [Garnett] don't like it, but am prepared. I shan't write in the same manner as *Sons and Lovers* again, I think—in that hard, violent style full of sensation and presentation. You must see what you think of the new style." And a month later he is stressing this same point with some very illuminating comments about the method of *Sons and Lovers:* ". . . I have no longer the joy in creating vivid scenes, that I had in *Sons and Lovers*. I don't care much more about accumulating objects in the powerful light of emotion, and making a scene of them. I have to write differently."

Finally, there is the well-known letter of June 5, 1914, in which Lawrence makes his most important statement about the newness of *The Rainbow*. In so doing he distinguishes this novel not only from *Sons and Lovers*, but also from the whole nineteenth-century tradition of character and social background:

You mustn't look in my novel for the old stable *ego*—of the character. There is another *ego*, according to whose action the individual is unrecognisable, and passes through, as it were, allotropic states which it needs a deeper sense than any we've been used to exercise, to discover are states of the same single radically unchanged element. (Like as diamond and coal are the same pure single element of carbon. The ordinary novel would trace the history of the diamond—but I say, 'Diamond, what! This is carbon.' And my diamond might be coal or soot, and my theme is carbon.) You must not say my novel is shaky—it is not perfect, because I am not expert in what I want to do. But it is the real thing, say what you like. And I shall get my reception, if not now, then before long. Again I say, don't look for the development of the novel to follow the lines of certain characters: the characters fall into the form of some other rhythmic form, as when one draws a fiddle-bow across a fine tray delicately sanded, the sand takes lines unknown.

The letters thus provide clear evidence that Lawrence believed *The Rainbow* to be a radical departure from his earlier work. The impression one gets from the novel bears this out, though not in such an obvious way as one might expect. The difference between *The Rainbow* and *Sons and Lovers* is not, for example, like that between *Ulysses* and *A Portrait of the Artist as a Young Man*. There are no new devices of technique which startle and puzzle the reader until he gets accustomed to them. The reader may very well progress some thirty or forty pages into *The Rainbow* before realizing that he is in fact encountering something radically different from what he has met in Lawrence's previous work.

The structure of *The Rainbow* is comparatively simple. The novel moves in temporal sequence through three generations of the Brangwen family, focusing in each generation on the relations between a man and a woman—Tom and Lydia, Will and Anna, and Ursula and Anton Skrebensky. The first two generations follow roughly parallel courses, and evolve roughly satisfactory relationships. In the last generation one person, Ursula, rather than an equally balanced couple, becomes the center of attention; and the narrative becomes her psychological odyssey. Impinging on each generation is the theme of the individual's need to feel in touch with the unknown, which gives the effect of crossing the clear temporal line of the novel's structure with a fainter, less definite one that is timeless. The analogies which this involves, unlike those between Joyce's epic and Homer's, are internal rather than external. The life struggle of one generation evokes comparisons with that of another. As Leavis comments, "It is the same life, and they are different lives, living differently the same problems—the same though different—in three interlinked generations." [1]

The reader fresh to *The Rainbow* might begin to feel after the first thirty or so pages that the novel is not getting anywhere, that no "story" is emerging. The characters, the social background, and, above all, the atmosphere are there; but not the tale that they usually adorn. What Lawrence is doing, one gradually realizes, with the nineteenth-century novel is very much like what Wordsworth did in *The Prelude* with the traditional epic. He is depriving it of its solidly objective narrative framework and substituting something introspective. What was normally regarded as the skeleton has gone, and the flesh, though not left to collapse into a shapeless mass, is given form by the imagination only. The personal coherence of the lyric replaces the narrative framework of the novel.

Yet this process is not so far gone as it is in the novels of Virginia Woolf. Lawrence retains much more of the traditional material than she, and that material is of immense importance to him. (It would be a serious mistake to represent Virginia Woolf as purifying the Lawrentian experiment. She actually diminishes it by reducing it to a condition very much closer to mere prose lyricism, especially in *The Waves*.) The result is a novel which, as Lawrence himself says, "hasn't got hard outlines." It is, like *The Prelude,* molded to the contours of the mind; but it draws its material much more widely from man in society, closely and accurately observed.

II *The First Generation*

The Rainbow opens with one of the most celebrated passages in Lawrence's work—the description of the old way of life of the male Brangwens. This is a life in which man, beast, and non-animal Nature are all closely integrated; and the pervasively sexual terms in which it is described suggest that the central, unifying experience common to every manifestation of life is sex. The effect, however, is not narrowly restrictive. Sex for Lawrence is a principle of vitality, not merely a reproductive function, and is associated with an intuitive mode of apprehension. This is implicit in the imagery and pulse-imitating rhythm of the opening passage. The Brangwen way of life is brimming over with vitality and the sexual overtones in the language describing it enhance this effect. Its essential characteristic is "blood-intimacy"—identification of the human life-flow with the great life-flow of nature, uninterrupted by the abstractions of "mental consciousness."

The sexual imagery also points forward to the preoccupation throughout the novel with courtship and marriage and, of course, with sex in the narrower sense of the word. No doubt one of the reasons for the book's being banned so soon after it was published was that it contained scenes of physical intercourse which were presented too frankly for British public opinion in 1915. But these were not included by Lawrence with any pornographic or sensationalist intention. On the contrary, physical intercourse is only one manifestation of the much wider Lawrentian conception of sex, though necessarily the most intense and urgent manifestation for human beings; and its centrality to marriage (just how central is carefully explained by Lawrence in *Fantasia of the Unconscious*) naturally makes it occupy an important place in *The Rainbow*. It is never seen, however, as an end in itself or in isolation from the wider conception of sex.

The blood-intimacy of the male Brangwens stands for something which has a deep appeal for Lawrence. With certain qualifications (to be developed in a moment) it can be regarded as his pastoral ideal—a Golden Age—by comparison with which modern life is a fallen condition. The Fall is represented and analyzed in the main body of the novel. The first two generations achieve a relationship in which sex is a great and revered mystery, but in neither case is it completely successful. There is an impression of decline in so far as Tom and Lydia settle for a compromise which, though satisfying, leaves them with less than the fully integrated life of the original ideal; and the relationship between Will and Anna, achieved only after much antagonism between them, is less stable than that of Tom and Lydia, and involves much greater sacrifice of potential development. The attempt at creating a true relationship in the third generation ends in a failure highlighted by the collapse of Skrebensky as a lover in the last terrible scene on the moonlit Lincolnshire beach; but this scene has much wider implications for the whole of modern society.

The "pastoral ideal" is, however, less than the full, complex ideal forming the standard by which criticism operates in *The Rainbow*. When Lawrence follows the description of the male life with the sentence,

Then the men sat by the fire in the house where the women moved about with surety, and the limbs and the body of the men were impregnated with the day, cattle and earth and vegetation and the sky, the men sat by the fire and their brains were inert, as their blood flowed heavy with the accumulation from the living day.   (Chap. 1) the reader's impression is mixed, as it is intended to be. The phrases "impregnated with the day, cattle and earth and vegetation" and "the accumulation from the living day" carry over the rich positives of the previous paragraph, but they are qualified by the phrase "their brains were inert" and by the curiously ambiguous word "heavy." Moreover, the statement that here in the house is the place "where the women moved about with surety" gives the faint suggestion that their menfolk on the contrary are ill at ease, out of their natural element. These are hints which serve as a bridge to the next paragraph dealing with the quite different feelings of the Brangwen women. They too feel "the drowse of blood-intimacy," but they demand a more varied conscious life: "But the women looked out from the heated, blind intercourse of farm-life, to the spoken world beyond. They were aware of the lips and the mind of the world speaking and giving utterance, they heard the sound in the distance, and they strained to listen." The women are attracted by the outside world. Their part of the farm faces out "to the road and the village with church and Hall and the world beyond." They are aware of the lips and the mind of the world speaking and giving finement of mind for which it is a symbol. They crave the "higher being" for their children, and for its achievement they look to education.

Blood-intimacy of the man, conscious awareness and education of the woman balance one another. Lawrence is not offering them as essentially male and female characteristics (in his work as a whole the roles of the two sexes are more frequently reversed), but as complementary to one another in a really satisfyingly human way of life. The male and the female in the Brangwens joined together constitute the implicit standard of *The Rainbow*. Yet, even so, there is a sense in which the intuitive integration of the earlier Brangwen men is more than a partner to the conscious striving of the women. It is a condition of vitality, a fundamental requirement of life in a way that the female aspiration is not. The Fall is in part caused by the female desire to venture beyond the narrow bounds of the Marsh Farm. (It is related to Lawrence's interpretation of the Fall of Man as due to the demand for knowledge.)

The later struggle of Ursula, who more than any other major character in *The Rainbow* has the opportunity of wider knowledge and education, is to recover the lost blood-intimacy, to save herself from the overdeveloped consciousness that atrophies the old intuitive life. Through her Lawrence communicates his own horror of the ashy condition to which life can be reduced by insisting upon knowledge as the chief end of man. Her meditation on the true relationship between the small circle of consciousness and the great, fecund outer darkness is one of the great value-stating passages in *The Rainbow:*

That which she was, positively, was dark and unrevealed, it could not come forth. It was like a seed buried in dry ash. This world in which she lived was like a circle lighted by a lamp. This lighted area, lit up by man's completest consciousness, she thought was all the world: that here all was disclosed for ever. Yet all the time, within the darkness she had been aware of points of light, like the eyes of wild beasts, gleaming, penetrating, vanishing. And her soul had acknowledged in a great heave of terror only the outer darkness. This inner circle of light in which she lived and moved, wherein the trains rushed and the factories ground out their machine-produce and the plants and the animals worked by the light of science and knowledge, suddenly it seemed like the area under an arc-lamp, wherein the moths and children played in the security of blinding light, not even knowing there was any darkness, because they stayed in the light.
But she could see the glimmer of dark movement just out of range, she saw the eyes of the wild beast gleaming from the darkness, watching the vanity of the camp fire and the sleepers; she felt the strange, foolish vanity of the camp, which said 'Beyond our light and our order there is nothing. . . .'
Nevertheless the darkness wheeled round about, with grey shadow-shapes of wild beasts, and also with dark shadow-shapes of the angels, whom the light fenced out, as it fenced out the more familiar beasts of darkness. And some, having for a moment seen the darkness, saw it bristling with the tufts of the hyaena and the wolf; and some, having given up their vanity of the light, having died in their own conceit, saw the gleam in the eyes of the wolf and the hyaena, that it was the flash of the sword of angels, flashing at the door to come in, that the angels in the darkness were lordly and terrible and not to be denied, like the flash of fangs. (Chap. 15)

Tom Brangwen is close to the type of the male Brangwen evoked at the beginning of the novel. His mother wishes him to be educated, and she sends him to the grammar school. But study is not in his nature: "In feeling he was developed, sensitive to the atmosphere around him, brutal perhaps, but at the same time delicate," but he knew "that his brain was a slow hopeless good-for-nothing." He has inherited the Brangwen regard for woman as the representative of the "higher being," and so his first experience of sex with a prostitute comes as a shock to him. It makes him more aware, however, of what he needs from woman: satisfaction of his deepest feelings, not mere physical relief. A later affair with a girl at Matlock is more remarkable for the man with whom it brings him into contact than for the girl herself. He is a foreigner and a gentleman, thus doubly mysterious and attractive to Tom. The encounter encourages him "to imagine an intimacy with fine-textured, subtle-mannered people such as the foreigner at Matlock, and amidst this subtle intimacy was always the satisfaction of a voluptuous woman." He becomes a romantic in his desires, refusing to be content with the life he knows; and, since the reality around him does not change, he takes to drink to drown reality. These drunken bouts are a parody of the original blood-intimacy. They give him a cheap "satisfaction," but leave him still with the problem of how to achieve a real and lasting satisfaction in his normal day-to-day existence.

He finds his answer in Lydia, a Polish widow, whose voluptuousness and foreignness together realize the dream which has begun to form within him. Tom's proposal to Lydia is one of a number of scenes which show that "sensation and presentation," despite Lawrence's comment on the difference between this novel and *Sons and Lovers,* are not absent from *The Rainbow.* There is a difference in quality nonetheless. The real interest is not now in the drama of the dialogue but in the flow of feeling communicated by the interpolated commentary. Possibly this is what Lawrence meant by saying, "It is all analytical."

'I came up,' he said, speaking curiously matter-of-fact and level, 'to ask if you'd marry me. You are free, aren't you?'

There was a long silence, whilst his blue eyes, strangely impersonal, looked into her eyes to seek an answer to the truth. He was looking for the truth out of her. And she, as if hypnotised, must answer at length.

'Yes, I am free to marry.'

The expression of his eyes changed, became less impersonal, as if he were looking almost at her, for the truth of her. Steady and intent and eternal they were, as if they would never change. They seemed to fix and to resolve her. She quivered, feeling herself created, will-less lapsing into him, into a common will with him.

'You want me?' she said.

A pallor came over his face.

'Yes,' he said.

Still there was a suspense and silence.

'No,' she said, not of herself. 'No, I don't know.'

He felt the tension breaking up in him, his fists slackened, he was unable to move. He stood looking at her, helpless in his vague collapse. For the moment she had become unreal to him. Then he saw her come to him, curiously direct and as if without movement, in a sudden flow. She put her hand to his coat.

'Yes I want to,' she said. . . .   (Chap. 1)

The actual words spoken are trivial compared with the tide of emotion flowing through the lovers. Various phrases suggest that they are in the hands of a force greater than themselves— "strangely impersonal," "as if hypnotized," "will-less," "not of herself"—but the scene as a whole does not produce a fatalistic impression. Rather, one feels that this is a moment when deeper levels than those of ordinary judgment and choice are reached. It confirms (though it is not the most remarkable example) Lawrence's claim that in *The Rainbow* characters do not govern development, but rather "fall into the form of some other rhythmic form."

Lydia's first husband had been older than she. Tom is younger. The first husband had borne her along in his wake, almost as a servant. Tom is more the deferential inferior, but he offers her the rooted stability that her first husband with his revolutionary fervor could not. She thus has a more balanced experience than Tom, and this frees her from the tension and anxiety that he feels. Yet the very foreignness that Tom finds so deeply attractive in her puts a distance between them. During her pregnancy, his desire cannot stand the test of her remoteness from him; and, when a visit to his brother's mistress again throws up the image of the romantically foreign in the form this time of a woman of culture and moral detachment, his wife senses his alienation. This particular form of foreignness is an illusion, an escape from the exacting challenge of creating a true relationship with his wife. At the same time it exposes a weakness in his attitude towards Lydia. Not knowing her had been an excuse for not being aware of her. "You only leave me alone or take me like your cattle, quickly, to forget me again—so that you can forget me again," says Lydia.

This conflict between them precedes an important progression in their relationship. Lawrence's "analytical" prose now becomes rather strained as he seeks to communicate the new, deeper love that wells up in Tom, annihilating the old dependent self and giving him a new independence which is also a capacity to realize the independent reality of his wife. Although doctrine is not fully transmuted into art, the passage is not altogether a failure. The very seriousness of what Lawrence is trying to communicate compels the reader to make allowances. One feels an urgent meaning struggling to break the bounds of language, and enough is achieved to make the new level of passion between Tom and Lydia convincing, if not completely coherent. This new love is an indication that they have at last forged their essential marriage. They now become independent pillars meeting "to the span of the heavens," with Lydia's daughter, Anna, representative of the next generation, confident and "free to play in the space beneath, between." Theirs is the first "rainbow" of the novel.

III *The Second Generation*

Tom Brangwen manages to achieve some degree of emotional stability, and this is primarily the outcome of his struggle to adjust himself to his wife Lydia. But his relationship with Anna also plays a part. The child is at first insecure and resentful of the strange new circumstances in which she finds herself after the marriage of her mother to Tom, and the effort which the latter makes to gain acceptance by the child is therapeutic for himself as well as for her. His ability to respond to his wife when she makes her challenge that he should recognize her as an independent being has, in fact, been cultivated by the simple necessity of winning over the child's confidence. The scenes which express this process are particularly alive. Their climax is the scene in which Tom, to quiet Anna when she is crying blindly for her mother, takes her with him to feed the cows. As they enter the barn it is like entering another world. The atmosphere is warm and heavy with the presence of cattle. Tom repeats the actions of shoveling the grain and carrying it to the cows in a rhythm faintly reminiscent of that natural pulselike rhythm which is part of the early Brangwen blood-intimacy, and it is the rhythm which seems finally to still the child.

The connection which is finally established between stepfather and daughter is deeper than that between the father and his own sons. There is clearly a sexual element in it, though without being in any way incestuous. The love which Tom feels for the girl is more than paternally protective. Without competing with the relationship being molded with his wife, it nevertheless provides a satisfaction for his deepest impulses which it could not do if it were not, in the Lawrentian sense, to some extent sexual. The precise quality of the relationship is difficult to convey. It is certainly such that, when Anna falls in love with Will Brangwen, Tom becomes jealous of a rival—though he succeeds in mastering his jealousy. But unlike Mrs. Morel's love for Paul, Tom's love for Anna does not undermine her independence and her ability to respond wholly to a lover. This is because Lydia is in no such position as Walter Morel. She remains central to Tom's life, with the result that Anna does not have to bear the same unnatural burden as Paul. In the end, when Tom wrestles with his jealousy over Anna, he is forced to admit to himself that it is his relationship with his wife that has been the one great achievement of his life: "What had he known, but the long, marital embrace with his wife! Curious, that this was what his life amounted to! At any rate, it was something, it was eternal . . . he was proud of it" (Chap. 4).

As the center of interest shifts from Tom and Lydia to Will and Anna, the mode of the novel becomes more and more one of dialectical opposition. Tom and Lydia, two people of very different character and background, had been drawn together by the attraction of opposites, and they were able, after conflict, to achieve a relationship in which they were not so much opposed as complementary to each other. Anna and Will are also temperamentally unlike, but their unlikeness produces such exacerbated conflict that only the sheer strength of their subterranean attraction for each other can hold them together.

The battle between them is the dominant thing, and they are equally matched. Anna is a thorough individualist who has no desire to take her stand on anything but her intrinsic personal quality (until the conflict dies down, that is). Will tries to take a stand on his importance as a man with a job to do in the outside world, but Anna's refusal to recognize his extramarital status soon makes him give up this attempt. They are both forced back on their own resources and made to enact a strictly individual dualism.

Their conflict is expressed in several finely observed domestic scenes, which again show Lawrence's continuing command of traditional realism when it suits his purposes; but it is through symbolic episodes that their conflict receives its most comprehensive expression. Two such episodes are of outstanding importance, and they both occur comparatively early in the development of the relationship, for it is in the early stages that the conflict is most fierce. Later the fires die down and there is some kind of truce between the lovers. Both episodes raise issues that take one beyond the immediate experience being communicated, and the second one in particular (the Lincoln Cathedral episode) is a central symbol for the whole novel. It connects the Will and Anna experience with what has gone before and with what is to come.

The first episode belongs to the courtship of Will and Anna. One evening during harvest time they put up sheaves together in a field of stubble while "A large gold moon hung heavily to the grey horizon." The moon, as so often in Lawrence's work, has a strange, electric power. It transforms the familiar landscape, and it forms an uncanny bond between Anna, Will, and the field in which they work. Repetition, with variation—as in Lawrence's poetry—to which the prose comes very close in this passage—produces an hypnotic effect, a gradually deepening vortex that draws the imagination down into a layer of meaning below that of ordinary consciousness. A rhythmical effect, similar to the passage describing Anna as a child in the cowshed with Tom, is achieved as the couple move to and fro carrying their sheaves, and it is intensified by the recurrent references to the moon which grows brighter and clearer as the rhythm of work gradually draws the two lovers together. The whole passage is an indirect evocation of sexual consummation—it is a development from, though much superior to, the indirectly sexual description of *The Trespasser*—and, even more strongly than the cowshed passage in this novel, recalls the sexuality which pervades man, beast, and nature in the Brangwens' pastoral ideal. The consummation (physical intercourse does not, apparently, take place, but the experience is nevertheless that of sexual consummation) is also the point at which the transmuting effect of the moon is highest and is accompanied by the fused sensations of suspension, surprise, increasing gentleness, and eternal stability. The experience is an imaginative leap outside time, but also a profoundly physical one which has a strong subterranean link with the original blood-intimacy. Having this dual aspect, it satisfies both Anna and Will.

The function of the sheaves episode is to underline the fundamental attraction, rooted in the Brangwen blood-intimacy, that makes the marriage of Anna and Will a true one. In their "ordinary" selves Anna and Will are irreconcilable. Will has a religious temperament—the religiousness of the artist, though, which is a profound desire for unity and harmony. Anna finds this suffocating. She demands something at once more sensibly immediate and less subject to order. She must, therefore, fight off Will's ecstasy by taunting and mocking it wherever it is vulnerable, especially where it takes the form of dogma which Will, having no theological equipment, or interest, cannot defend. The novel here touches upon the "new criticism" of the late nineteenth century, but the interest is not in the intellectual movement as such. The sceptical, agnostic tendencies of the time simply provide Anna with a weapon which she can use against the unwelcome pressures of Will's mystical temperament. In this aspect their conflict is a modified, and more maturely balanced, presentment of the conflict between Paul and Miriam in *Sons and Lovers;* for Anna's position agrees roughly with Paul's, and Miriam's (though here the modification is considerable) with Will's. There are, of course, several differences between the two couples which would make a comparison of them on the level of character ridiculous; but, in quality of mind—always with the proviso that the pair in *The Rainbow* is presented with more detachment and by a more mature artist—they are not dissimilar. The difference which is really important is that Will and Anna are able to supersede their conflict in sexual fulfillment. Neither, despite the frequent storminess of the marriage, is driven to the sexual split that afflicts Paul Morel.

Sons and Lovers is also recalled by the visit to Lincoln Cathedral. This episode is a much richer elaboration of the brief passage in the earlier novel in which Paul compares Miriam to Gothic architecture and himself to Norman. The cathedral for Will is an experience of timeless completeness, a "consummation" and a "rainbow." It is a symbol of wholeness, containing all opposites:

Away from time, always outside of time! Between east and west, between dawn and sunset, the church lay like a seed in silence, dark before germination, silenced after death. Containing birth and death, potential with all the noise and transitation of life, the cathedral remained hushed, a great, involved seed, whereof the flower would be radiant life inconceivable, but whose beginning and whose end were the circle of silence. Spanned round with the rainbow, the jewelled gloom folded music upon silence, light upon darkness, fecundity upon death, as a seed folds leaf upon leaf and silence upon the root and the flower, hushing up the secret of all between its parts, the death out of which it fell, the life into which it has dropped, the immortality it involves, and the death it will embrace again. (Chap. 7)

The nave, with its series of great, leaping arches, objectifies for Will his own ecstasy: "There his soul remained, at the apex of the arch, clinched in the timeless ecstasy, consummated." The soaring movement appeals to the female Brangwen element in him. It recalls the original contrast between the low, flat Marsh Farm and the church and town on the hill of Ilkeston. As the male Brangwen working on the "horizontal land" was "aware of something standing above him and beyond him in the distance," so the arches of the cathedral "leapt up from the plain of earth . . . away from the horizontal earth." But as the cathedral includes the horizontal as well, it is completely satisfying to Will.

For Anna it is not so. It is an "ultimate confine." The leaping away from the horizontal is not enough to satisfy her desire for prospects beyond. She seizes upon the mocking discordancies of the gargoyles and uses them as a weapon against Will's suffocating ecstasy, much as she uses her attacks on his dogma. Above all she wants the open sky and the sense that there is freedom beyond what appears to be the enclosing boundary. The image used for this is the natural one of the bird:

She wanted to get out of this fixed, leaping, forward-travelling movement, to rise from it as a bird rises with wet, limp feet from the sea, to lift herself as a bird lifts its breast and thrusts its body from the pulse and heave of a sea that bears it forward to an unwilling conclusion, tear herself away like a bird on wings, and in the open space where there is clarity, rise up above the fixed, surcharged motion, a separate speck that hangs suspended, moves this way and that, seeing and answering before it sinks again, having chosen or found the direction in which it shall be carried forward. (Chap. 7)

The bird represents the unfixed spontaneity of Nature as against the cathedral's pretension to completeness and permanency. It is an attitude which Lawrence endorses in many other of his writings, and it is not surprising that Anna wins a victory over her husband. The victory is only partial in that both are altered— "She had some new reverence for that which he wanted, he felt that his cathedrals would never again be to him as they had been"—but emphasis falls on the modifying of Will's ecstatic self-sufficiency rather than on Anna's "new reverence." The bird image is now used in connection with Will too, as he realizes that:

> Outside the cathedral were many flying spirits that could never be sifted through the jewelled gloom. He had lost his absolute.
>
> He listened to the thrushes in the gardens and heard a note which the cathedrals did not include: something free and careless and joyous. (Chap. 7)

His conclusion is not rejection of all that the cathedral stands for, but a transformation which is nevertheless profound: the laying open of the cathedral to the incalculable influences of Nature —"a temple was never perfectly a temple, till it was ruined and mixed up with the winds and the sky and the herbs."

As Patricia Abel and Robert Hogan have shown,[2] the bird, which has associations with fertility ritual obviously appropriate to the rejection of a would-be all-inclusive Christianity, is also used in a brief paragraph of the final chapter to describe the feelings of Anna's daughter, Ursula. Ursula enters a wood where the trees seem as if they "might turn and shut her in," and then she escapes into a meadow: "She felt like a bird that has flown in through the window of a hall where vast warriors sit at the board. Between their grave, booming ranks she was hastening, assuming she was unnoticed, till she emerged, with beating heart, through the far window and out into the open, upon the vivid green, marshy meadow" (Chap. 16).

This image emphasizes the connection between mother and daughter. Ursula has the same instinct as Anna to reject any system of all-enclosing self-sufficiency. Nevertheless, her experience is not simply a repetition of her mother's. In the passage just quoted there is an interesting variation of their common image in that the bird flies with relief into "the vivid green, marshy meadow." This as naturally recalls the Marsh Farm as the bird itself recalls Anna's desire for freedom. Ursula's experience is to lead her to distrust a society which is dedicated to the utmost increase of mental consciousness, and for her the natural reaction will be *away* from the critical intellect and *towards* renewal of the ancient blood-intimacy. The daughter will not be more in the right, however, than the mother. No single ideal will be made to prevail. What Lawrence values is the flexibility prompting the reactions of both Anna and Ursula. Neither of them believes in a system for the sake of which she makes her fierce struggles. They both have a surer instinct of rejection than of acceptance, and in each we can see the true nonconformist's determination not to rest in the authority of an established wisdom that does not satisfy her deepest needs.

To return, however, to the second generation of loves, the episode of Lincoln Cathedral is a crucial experience in the lives of both Anna and Will: "They went home again, both of them altered." It is also an apex from which they decline, for neither is quite so intense again. With a gradual abatement of conflict in their marriage goes a lessening of its visionary quality. Will accepts an unadventurous existence, with occasional blind rages, and with at times a tragic quality about him: "He was aware of some limit to himself, of something unformed in his very being, of some buds which were not ripe in him, some folded centres of darkness which would never develop and unfold whilst he was alive in the body" (Chap. 7). Anna lets herself sink into motherhood. She acknowledges nothing but her own pregnancies and her own feeding of her babies. The sexual bond between husband and wife is not broken, but, in a sense, it stagnates.

No further creativeness comes of their marriage. This, perhaps, is the significance of Anna's cult of her own motherhood. She has given up the creative effort in itself, and made herself simply the channel for new life. Will does make attempts to use his artistic gifts again, but he finds that his best things are merely reproductive. In the end he satisfies himself by becoming a handicraft instructor. Both husband and wife relapse into secondary roles, leaving the primary adventure and conflict of life to their offspring.

IV   *The Third Generation*

The section devoted to Ursula and to the third generation is the longest in the book. There are various reasons for this. The problems of the earlier generations come to a head in this one, and Ursula herself is a more complicated person than any of her forebears. She has something of Anna's temperament, but she also inherits Will's religious sense and is in revolt against her mother's preoccupation with childbearing. In Ursula the blood of the Brangwens and the Polish blood of her mother and grandmother are mixed. What has hitherto been a dualism, roughly expressed in marriages of two opposite types of human being, becomes in Ursula a more complex mingling. She is reminiscent of her grandparents as well as of her mother and father. Lydia is the person for whom she has most respect, but she also shares Tom's unconscious allegiance to the Marsh Farm and all that it stands for. Ursula is the meeting point of several different strands in the Brangwen tradition, and her life is the one in which that tradition is exposed to the destructive forces of modern civilization.

This section of the novel is also the one in which most attention is given to adolescence. Ursula goes through a more prolonged adolescence than any of the earlier characters, or at least she appears to. Her education, which is also much more extensive, is in part responsible for this. Higher education prolongs, and thereby enriches, the period of growth; but, in doing so, it retards the transition from adolescence to the (comparative) emotional stability of adulthood. At least this is the case with Ursula. Her life is crowded with a wider range of experience than falls to any other character, but it is also more emotionally turbulent. She is a restless, difficult, egocentric young woman, rather too liberally endowed with the Lawrentian cocksureness (she is at times dangerously near to being simply an *alter ego*), but she is always an interesting person.

Ursula, like Peer Gynt, is an ultra-romantic who is forced to peel off layer after layer of illusion. She begins, as a girl, with a fairy-tale romanticism, which is succeeded by a religious mysticism inherited from her father. This mysticism breaks down when the artificial distinction between "a weekday world of people and trains and duties and reports" and "a Sunday world of absolute truth and living mystery" can no longer satisfy her. Two love affairs follow, one with the schoolmistress, Winifred Inger, and one with Anton Skrebensky. The latter is, of course, more important than the Lesbian flirtation with Miss Inger, which is less significant in itself than for the new ideas which it introduces to Ursula. Miss Inger is interested in scientific materialism and in the rights of women, both subjects for which Lawrence has an intense dislike. She represents the association of mental and emotional forms of perversion, and the pattern of corruption is completed when she later marries Ursula's Uncle Tom, the manager of a horribly degraded Yorkshire colliery, who has similar intellectual interests.

Ursula's relationship with Anton Skrebensky, which actually begins before her affair with Miss Inger, is dropped when Skrebensky goes to fight in the Boer War, but it is resumed while Ursula is a student at University College, Nottingham. The first part of the relationship is different from the second, because initially Skrebensky is able to satisfy Ursula's physical demand and she is content with a primarily physical satisfaction. But already there are suggestions that he is not an adequate mate for Ursula. He cannot convince her that his life as a soldier has any real meaning for him, and he is diffident about the quality of his love for her. This is revealed by their meeting with a bargeman whose admiration for Ursula makes Skrebensky conscious of his own inadequacy:

He was envying the lean father of three children, for his impudent directness and his worship of the woman in Ursula, a worship of body and soul together, the man's body and soul wistful and worshipping the body and spirit of the girl, with a desire that knew the inaccessibility of its object, but was only glad to know that the perfect thing existed, glad to have had a moment of communion.

Why could not he himself desire a woman so? Why did he never really want a woman, not with the whole of him: never love, never worship, only just physically want her?   (Chap. 11)

The bargeman is only a minor character on the fringe of the novel—he is a prototype of, for example, the gypsy in *The Virgin and the Gipsy*—but he is sufficiently realized to define what is essentially lacking in Skrebensky. Even when at his best in loving Ursula, Skrebensky is circumscribed. He can only achieve a sense of "maximum self, in contradistinction to all the rest of life." There is a great scene at a wedding held at Marsh Farm when he makes love to Ursula "in the overwhelming luminosity of the moon." The setting is inevitably reminiscent of the earlier scene between Will and Anna, but what it produces is utterly different. In her moment of rapture Ursula is destructive, the *vulva denticulata:* "fierce, corrosive, seething with his destruction, seething like some cruel, corrosive salt around the last substance of his being." She exposes him—and the moon, for Lawrence, is the inevitable accompanying symbol—to an ultra-human experience which shatters his ordinary, limited humanity.

When Skrebensky returns from South Africa, their affair enters its critical phase. Ursula's intervening experience—her affair with Miss Inger, her two years as a teacher, and her studies at the college—has given her a profound disillusion with education. The one study that is still meaningful to her is biology which intensifies her sense of the mystery of life. The rest seems an arrogant assertion of mental consciousness and fundamentally materialistic. Skrebensky is already partially identified for her with the society on which this system of education is based (he is its unthinking defender), and she now unconsciously treats him as its embodiment and challenges him to the impossible task of transcending its limitations.

In this more than in the previous sections of *The Rainbow* the characters must be read as agents rather than controllers of the novel's development. Skrebensky is no longer a person with this or that characteristic who is making this or that choice. He is a lover—as Shakespeare's Romeo or Antony are lovers—but he is crippled in his capacity for love by the nature of the society which he accepts—and from which he springs. In this respect he is the forerunner both of Gerald in *Women in Love* and of Sir Clifford in *Lady Chatterley's Lover* (but he is a better realization of the idea than Sir Clifford because his crippling remains psychic). The test to which he is put is sexual, but, again, the standard of sexuality is that which Lawrence has set up within the novel and realized in the couples of the two previous generations. Anton's failure, which is more than a matter of physical inadequacy, though it also becomes that, is defined when Ursula realizes that "She knew him all round, not on any side did he lead into the unknown." The disastrous culmination of their affair is the final lovemaking on the Lincolnshire beach, with the moon once again ironically presiding:

. . . She lay motionless, with wide-open eyes looking at the moon. He came direct to her, without preliminaries. She held him pinned down at the chest, awful. The fight, the struggle for consummation was terrible. It lasted till it was agony to his soul, till he succumbed, till he gave way as if dead, and lay with his face buried, partly in her hair, partly in the sand, motionless, as if he would be motionless now for ever, hidden away in the dark, buried, only buried, he only wanted to be buried in the goodly darkness, only that, and no more.

He seemed to swoon. It was a long time before he came to himself. He was aware of an unusual motion of her breast. He looked up. Her face lay like an image in the moonlight, the eyes wide open, rigid. But out of the eyes, slowly, there rolled a tear, that glittered in the moonlight as it ran down her cheek.

He felt as if the knife were being pushed into his already dead body. With head strained back, he watched, drawn tense, for some minutes, watched the unaltering, rigid face like metal in the moonlight, the fixed, unseeing eyes, in which slowly the water gathered, shook with glittering moonlight, then surcharged, brimmed over and ran trickling, a tear with its burden of moonlight, into the darkness, to fall in the sand.   (Chap. 15)

Lawrence's earlier title for this novel was *The Wedding Ring* which is more appropriate to the central theme than *The Rainbow*. Marriage is here presented as the most serious experience of human life. Tom Brangwen's drunken discourse at the wedding of Will and Anna is a parody of this concept, but the theme is solidly enough embedded in the novel for it to stand parody. The relationship between Ursula and Skrebensky does not issue in marriage because Skrebensky cannot make himself a husband for Ursula, and the triviality of his subsequent marriage to his colonel's daughter emphasizes the hollowness of his conception of marriage. He is the last and greatest of Ursula's disillusionments. Instead of being one of the mythical Sons of God, as she had imagined him, he is a puny modern, dwarfed by the giant race before the Flood represented by Tom and Will Brangwen. The Flood which drowns Tom comes chronologically after the marriages of the first two generations, dividing them from the unavailing attempt at a marriage between Skrebensky and Ursula, and so gives a symbolic heightening to the failure of the third generation. The balance of blood-intimacy and the beyond is lost and, with it, the foundation on which an essential marriage can be built.

V   *The Ending: Ursula's Vision of the Horses*

Lawrence could have ended the novel here, but he adds the final section in which Ursula has her terrifying encounter with the horses, and then, after recovery from illness, is given her "rainbow" as the promise of "a new growth." The horses are a peculiarly inscrutable symbol. The power and terror that they communicate give the episode an hallucinatory or dreamlike quality.

The horse symbol is a frequent one in Lawrence, and its appearance in dreams fascinated him so much that he devoted a
very interesting passage in *Fantasia of the Unconscious* to ex-
plaining it:

> . . . the horse-dream refers to some arrest in the deepest sensual
> activity in the male. The horse is presented as an object of terror,
> which means that to the man's automatic dream-soul, which loves
> automatism, the great sensual male activity is the greatest menace. The
> automatic pseudo-soul, which has got the sensual nature repressed,
> would like to keep it repressed. Whereas the greatest desire of the liv-
> ing spontaneous soul is that this very male sensual nature, represented
> as a menace, shall be actually accomplished in life. The spontaneous
> self is secretly yearning for the liberation and fulfilment of the deepest
> and most powerful sensual nature.[3]

This also provides an excellent comment on the horse symbol as
it appears at the end of *The Rainbow*. The sense of repression
is powerfully communicated in the description of "their breasts
gripped, clenched narrow in a hold that never relaxed" and of
". . . their haunches, so rounded, so massive, pressing, pressing,
pressing to burst the grip upon their breasts, pressing forever till
they went mad, running against the walls of time, and never
bursting free" (Chap. 16). The horses are driven mad by repression, yet can never wholly be repressed, for, the description
continues, "the darkness and wetness of rain could not put out the
hard, urgent, massive fire that was locked within these flanks,
never, never."

And, certainly, Lawrence communicates the sense that "the
spontaneous self" in Ursula "is secretly yearning for the liberation
and fulfillment of the deepest and most powerful sensual nature,"
which—in the terms of this novel—is the old Brangwen blood-
intimacy. In this paradox of repression and the irrepressible lies
the hope that can be extended at the end.

The counterpart in the actual world of "the walls of time"
against which the horses strain is the tyranny of mental consciousness, the disease of the third, or modern, generation—suggested more concretely at the end of the novel by the rash of
hard, raw buildings that is spreading over the Derbyshire countryside. The counterpart of the unquenchable "fire" of the horses, on
the other hand, is the rainbow which forms over the new houses
and reassures Ursula that the "people who crept hard-scaled and

separate on the face of the world's corruption were living still, that the rainbow was arched in their blood and would quiver to life in their spirit" (Chap. 16). This coda is not altogether convincing. The rainbow seems like wishful thinking rather than a promise inherent in the human experience which is presented in the bulk of the novel. Lawrence appears to be drawing the conclusion that he would like to draw—not the one which his imagination demands. His vision of "the earth's new architecture, the old, brittle corruption of houses and factories swept away" is without substance. The vision, however, of unquenchable energy embodied in the horses is not only compelling, but it is realized as an integral part of the whole work. This, instead of being something arbitrarily inserted at the end, is related to the blood-intimacy of the Brangwens; it is part of a consistent tradition running through the three generations; and it reaches its climax in Ursula. The world of the last generation has been submerged by a catastrophic Flood. Everything is reduced by mental consciousness to a brittle unreality. But the horses and Ursula's experience with them which clinches her refusal to accept this world offer some sort of hope for the future. Her divine discontent is a sign that the rainbow, though not made actual in a new society or a new marriage, is still "arched" in Ursula's Brangwen blood.

CHAPTER 4

Women in Love

I *The Real World and the World of Art*

Women *in Love* is a sequel to *The Rainbow*, continuing the story of Ursula's attempt to achieve a satisfactory love relationship, and bringing her sister, Gudrun, into new prominence. (Lawrence originally had it in mind to write one novel, not two, under the title *The Sisters.*) *Women in Love* is, however, a more artistically controlled novel than *The Rainbow*. Nowhere else does Lawrence achieve such an equable distribution of his creative powers. It can be praised on several grounds—for structural simplicity and toughness, for psychological penetration, for the ambitious presentation of men and women in relation to the forces of modern industrialism, and for its great scenes of untranslatable symbolic power. But it is the combining of all these in an organically related work of art that makes *Women in Love* such a remarkable achievement.

Lawrence will have nothing to do, however, with the notion of a work of art as an end in itself. For him art is necessarily connected with life, not a substitute for it. He sides with Ursula, who asserts that "The world of art is only the truth about the real world," against the decadent artist, Loerke, for whom a work of art is "a picture of nothing," having "nothing to do with anything but itself . . . no relation with the everyday world." And Loerke's point of view is disproved within the novel by its relationship to his own character, to Gudrun who agrees with him, and, more ambiguously, to Gudrun's lover, Gerald.

The work which provokes Ursula's criticism is Loerke's sculpture of "a massive, magnificent stallion, rigid with pent-up power" on which a slender, adolescent girl (Loerke's interpretation of Lady Godiva) is sitting sideways. The subject is one which has a clear significance to the reader familiar with Lawrence's work. The model whom Loerke used for Lady Godiva turns out to have been an art student who had been brutally treated by Loerke. He

chooses an adolescent because he finds women artistically un-
interesting after twenty. The suggestion of corruption which
emerges from these details about his approach to his art is confirmed by the part he plays in the action of the novel, especially
by his mesmeric effect on Gudrun and by his share in the destruction of Gerald.

The connection between the sculpture and the novel as a whole
is further underlined by Gerald's contribution to the discussion.
His reactions have the confusion of a divided mind. At first he
appears to side against Ursula, but he exposes himself to the
sneers of Gudrun by suggesting that Loerke has got his legend
wrong. He assumes some sort of connection with life while Gudrun takes the extreme aesthetic view of Loerke. The sharpest
contrast between them is provoked by the feet of the Godiva.
"Didn't he understand her!" exclaims Gudrun. "You've only to
look at the feet—aren't they darling, so pretty and tender." The
adjectives are drained of life. Like Loerke, she is willing to squeeze
adolescence dry and then discard it. To Gerald the feet suggest
"pathetic shyness and fear." He is at first "fascinated," then pained,
and then filled with a sense of "barrenness." That he is attracted
at all shows the degree to which he is infected by the corruption
of Gudrun and Loerke. (Gerald, the industrialist, is also related
to Loerke's factory fresco in which human beings are shown enjoying the sensation of being operated by machines.) But the
fact that he is instinctively repelled suggests the finer potentiality
that fails to be realized in him and makes his career a tragedy.

The self-substantial world that Lawrence creates in *Women in
Love* is thus not an isolated world. It is a parallel creation that
reflects and comments on reality. The criticism of industrial society which it contains is intended as a serious diagnosis of the
evils afflicting the real world, and the exploration of marriage—
a theme which is carried over from *The Rainbow*—makes close
demands on the reader's own understanding of the problems of
actual life. Indeed, the major weakness of *Women in Love* is
perhaps an overeagerness to tie the fictional to the real world,
involving a descent from the level of art to mere preaching.

Birkin, the man who becomes Ursula's lover and husband, is
rather too much of a preacher. He is given to dogmatic assertions
very much like those of Lawrence himself. Lawrence was well
aware of the dangers inherent in this. If he uses Birkin as a
mouthpiece for some of his own ideas, he also puts him up as a

target for satire, both by means of parody, as in the Pompadour scene where one of Birkin's ridiculously sermonlike letters is read aloud, and by subjecting him to straightforward attack from Ursula. One such attack reveals a very real weakness in Birkin-Lawrence and indicates a capacity for self-criticism that Lawrence is too little credited with. Pleading for spontaneity, Birkin says to Ursula: "I want you to trust yourself so implicitly, that you can let yourself go." Ursula's rejoinder is pointed: "*I* can let myself go, easily enough. It is you who can't let yourself go, it is you who hang on to yourself as if it were your only treasure. *You—you* are the Sunday school teacher—*You*—you preacher" (Chap. 19). The author comments: "The amount of truth that was in this made him stiff and unheeding of her."

A more drastic threat to the novel is that Lawrence's hammering out of a doctrine can sometimes cause him to substitute assertion for presentment. This particularly affects the curious relationship of *Blutbrüderschaft* which Birkin tries to establish with Gerald. Lawrence's own doubts about the possibility of such a male relationship are reflected in Ursula's criticism. To her it is merely a sign of Birkin's willfulness. But Lawrence persists with it, and in the end tries to make the reader believe that Gerald's tragedy results from his failure to respond to Birkin's offer, as well as from his failure with Gudrun. We are even told at the end of Chapter 25 that Gerald's failure with Gudrun could be averted if he accepted Birkin's offer first. The comment is a gratuitous intrusion by Lawrence of a private *idée fixe*.

Another, allied weakness is the failure to separate author from character sufficiently clearly. Gudrun and Ursula are characters in their own right. They do not invite confusion with their creator in the way that Birkin frequently does. But at times Lawrence presents their feelings and views so immediately that they seem to carry the full weight of the author's approval, even though this is detrimental to his general intentions. His style lives too much for the moment and not enough for the novel as a whole. Ursula, for example, at the beginning of Chapter 19 feels "contemptuous, resistant indifference" to the whole world. Although this reaction has primarily to do with the stage she has reached in her relationship with Birkin, and one can, therefore, read the passage as the rendering of a mood particular to one person at one time, there is no denying that Lawrence's prose seems to give her thoughts a much more permanent authority. Such passages give many readers the mistaken impression that Lawrence is writing from a basically misanthropic position.

None of these flaws, however, in *Women in Love* amounts to a major defect. The novel is great enough to carry them. If it is wrong to be merely uncritically admiring, it is equally unjust not to recognize the overriding richness of achievement in *Women in Love*.

II *Gerald and Birkin*

The basic device of *Women in Love* is comparison and contrast. The two couples, Birkin and Ursula, Gerald and Gudrun, together with Hermione, Birkin's former mistress, not only provide the main interest of the novel but are linked and contrasted in a variety of ways. Birkin is fundamentally opposed to modern industrial civilization. Through him Lawrence anticipates present-day criticism of the hunt for status symbols. Life is turned into "a blotch of labour," Birkin tells Gerald, "so that your collier can have a pianoforte in his parlour, and you can have a butler and a motor-car in your up-to-date house." Gerald, on the other hand, accepts "the plausible ethics of productivity." To this extent the two men are opposites.

Their relationship is, however, more complicated than this. Gerald is the son of a powerful mine owner, Thomas Crich, who, though a capitalist committed to ownership and dominance, is morally a Christian Socialist. He is split between love and power, unable wholly to commit himself to either, and practises a charity which has no real roots in himself. What Lawrence is interested in is the psychic penalty paid by Mr. Crich and his family for this worship of an impracticable ideal. One sees it clearly in the slightly crazed behavior of Gerald's mother, a creature whose instinctive haughtiness is smothered by her husband's charity. She is a caged hawk: "Strange, like a bird of prey, with the fascinating beauty and abstraction of a hawk, she had beat against the bars of his philanthropy, and like a hawk in a cage, she had sunk into silence" (Chap. 17).

This hawk imagery is transferred to Gerald, and it provides a clue to that aspect of his nature which is at odds with "the plausible ethics of productivity." Although he takes over his father's business, reorganizes the mines, and creates out of them a supremely efficient mechanism, he comes to this task only after a prolonged attempt to escape from industrialism. And, after completing the work so effectively that his own guidance is no longer necessary, he finds himself threatened by a terrifying inner emptiness: "He was afraid that one day he would break down and be a purely meaningless babble lapping round a darkness." He is even more deeply divided than his father, for life and death are in conflict within his very being. Handsome and vigorous, he is yet marked from boyhood as a Cain figure by his accidental killing of his brother; and his fair hair and white skin glistening "like sunshine refracted through crystals of ice" hint at the death which is to overtake him in the Austrian mountains.

This contrast within Gerald complicates the contrast between him and Birkin. The hint given in the hawk imagery of a link between Gerald and his mother allies him imaginatively with Birkin who is one of the few people whose existence Mrs. Crich recognizes. Gerald's inability to be satisfied with industrialism, although it is his conscious creed, suggests a fundamental kinship with Birkin. And there is a further strand to the relationship, making the contrast between them still less a matter of merely opposed ideas, in that Birkin, if not divided like Gerald, is still entangled in the destructive forces of which he is such a loud critic. Birkin's uncertainty is betrayed in the stridency with which he attacks his opponents, and the very arguments into which his heretical opinions draw him undermine his struggle to escape from the sterility he detests.

III *Birkin, Hermione, and Ursula*

The deadly sterile element in Birkin's life centers, however, upon his relationship with Hermione rather than with Gerald. As the novel begins, his affair with her is already coming to an end, but it still has something of a hold over him, and it is of considerable importance as indicating the kind of relationship that Birkin has cultivated in the past. Hermione is a cultured hostess who has a devouring interest in intellectual life. She is completely lacking in spontaneity, and everything for her is so forced into consciousness and so subjected to will that there is a total split in her between knowing and being which threatens to disintegrate her. There is a resemblance between her condition and the relapse suffered by Gerald after the completion of his reorganization of the mines, except that hers is a more advanced and habitual condition: "There always seemed an interval, a strange split between what she seemed to feel and experience, and what she actually said and thought. She seemed to catch her thoughts at length from off the surface of a maelstrom of chaotic black emotions and reactions, and Birkin was always filled with repulsion, she caught so infallibly, her will never failed her. Her voice was always dispassionate and tense, and perfectly confident" (Chap. 12).

Birkin, strong as his repulsion is, cannot quite cut himself off from Hermione. Nor, of course, is Hermione willing to let him. The capacity for free, spontaneous action which Birkin possesses, in spite of his excessive intellectualism, has become her substitute for life. She is one more variation on the constant theme in Lawrence of a clinging dependence—even though hidden by an appearance of confidence and self-control—that comes from a failure to achieve normal wholeness of being. The subterranean currents that control their relationship are felt in scene after scene of rudeness and disagreeableness between them, but do not really break the surface until Hermione's self-control snaps and she hurls a heavy paperweight at Birkin's head. This scene, which might have been comic, or melodramatic, is neither; for it is presented as the culmination of a long, festering relationship. The scene immediately following, in which Birkin strips off his clothes in the woods and rolls among the wet leaves, does strike one as queer and slightly comic, but at least the revulsion from human society which prompts it is made understandable.

The woman to whom Birkin turns as a relief from the relationship with Hermione is Ursula. These two women have not only different characters and temperaments but also different life principles. Ursula is a creature of impulse rather than of deliberate will. She has a natural affinity with all living things. Both she and Gudrun, for example, are horrified by Gerald's treatment of his horse at the beginning of Chapter 9 (he forces it to stand and endure the noise of a clanking coal train at a level crossing), but it is Ursula who is the more outraged.

In her relationship with Birkin she is put in the paradoxical situation of being made an offer of marriage by a man whom she instinctively likes, but on terms that she instinctively rejects. In the end she accepts him seemingly on the spur of the moment. They have a tremendous row in which Birkin accuses her of being obsessed with the benevolent ideal of "love," which is really an expression of her female conceit, and Ursula accuses him of egotism and male conceit. At the climax Ursula throws back at him the rings he has given her and walks off. Unlike Hermione, whose will power involves a deadly suppression of her true feelings, Ursula speaks her mind bluntly, and this makes the quarrel a catharsis which purges all the differences causing surface conflict between the two lovers, but leaves the permanent bond between them unbroken. She comes back in a penitent mood, and she and Birkin are reconciled. What follows is neither the triumph of her notion of "love," nor her conversion to his doctrine of marriage, but her acceptance of their mutual bond. Lawrence is trying to suggest that, although Birkin may be more in the right about what is a suitable basis for marriage than Ursula, her decision has to come from her whole being. She cannot be argued into submission.

IV *Gudrun*

Ursula's sister, Gudrun, is the strangest of the major characters in the novel. She is in many ways like Ursula: they are both proud, sensitive, independent creatures, sisters in spirit as well as in blood. A very intimate relationship exists between them. Gudrun, however, is the more self-contained. At the very beginning of the book, when the two women are sitting talking, this quality in Gudrun draws admiration from her sister: "She thought Gudrun so *charming,* so infinitely charming, in her softness and her fine, exquisite richness of texture and delicacy of line. There was a certain playfulness about her too, such a piquancy or ironic suggestion, such an untouched reserve" (Chap. 1).

But this passage expresses only a part of Lawrence's intention with regard to Gudrun. The dialogue between her and Ursula reveals more. Gudrun says things with a chilling, repressive effect. She pretends to be detached even when she is moved. Already she is an exile from her native Derbyshire returning "new from her life in Chelsea and Sussex," and she carries a slight taint of self-conscious culture and sophistication which makes her reject the mining area in which she was brought up. Nevertheless, it has a queer attraction for her. She finds the voices of the miners "full of an intolerable deep resonance, like a machine's burring, a music more maddening than the siren's long ago."

Gudrun's reaction to the miners suggests a connection with the dissolute world of the Bohemian dilettante, Halliday, and his mistress, Minette, to which at certain stages both Birkin and Gerald are drawn. The symbol of that world is the African stat-

uette, representing the lapse of "the desire for creation and pro-
ductive happiness" and its replacement by "mindless progressive
knowledge through the senses . . . mystic knowledge in disintegration and dissolution, knowledge such as the beetles have,
which live purely within the world of corruption and cold dissolution" (Chap. 19). This is the African form of the destructive
process. The white races are destined to "fulfil a mystery of ice-
destructive knowledge, snow-abstract annihilation," as Gerald
ultimately does. But the process is the same: a disintegration of
the complex balance of the psyche demanded by the ideal of
wholeness.

V *Gudrun, Gerald, and the Way of Disintegration*

The novel offers the four main characters a choice between this
process of disintegration and a marriage based on "polarity."
The latter way is accepted by Ursula and Birkin. For Ursula this
leads to the fulfillment of a desire which reaches back into the
earlier part of her life recorded in *The Rainbow:* Birkin becomes
to her what Skrebensky failed to be—one of the "Sons of God."
For Birkin, Ursula, who has always been an embodiment of the
spontaneity which he admires, becomes the woman who can release the spontaneity in himself which Hermione and his own
intellectualism have thwarted. There is a weakness in the development of this theme in so far as *Women in Love* is a novel of
courtship rather than of marriage proper; but, as F.R. Leavis
maintains, enough is shown of their relationship to demonstrate
its success and to make a significant contrast with the disastrous
failure of Gerald and Gudrun. The affair between these two does
not end in marriage. Gudrun refuses marriage outright, and
Gerald's willingness to submit to the institutional aspect of marriage, while leaving the real relationship to lead a shameful
"subterranean" existence, only emphasizes his inability to realize
what true marriage entails. They, in effect, choose the way of disintegration, with the sinister, obscene kind of excitement which
it offers.

In seeking to convey the quality of the experience shared by
Gerald and Gudrun, Lawrence faces one of his most difficult
problems as a novelist. His solution is the creation of powerful
symbolic scenes, such as that in which Gudrun dances before the
Highland cattle, in which the sinister element in Gudrun herself
and in her relationship with Gerald are not described but im-

mediately communicated. Part of the Highland cattle scene can be explained: the cattle belong to Gerald, they are bullocks, and Gudrun's dance is, therefore, tantamount to a denial of his male potency. But what gives the scene its imaginative power, as Eliseo Vivas maintains, is the "fascinating but obscure something that teases but does not yield to any kind of clear grasp." [1] The very quality in the Gudrun-Gerald relationship which makes it disastrous is here involved. Vivas, penetrating as his discussion of this scene is, still queries Gudrun's motive for wanting to destroy Gerald; but this is to demand an explanation of the sort that Lawrence's art renders superfluous. Attempting to consider the scene in isolation, of course, creates further difficulty. The Highland cattle episode is part of the total presentation of the corruption affecting Gudrun and, through her, Gerald. It has an internal coherence and consistency with the rest of the novel which are far more important than any rationalizing could be.

Another symbolic episode, which deepens the implications of this one of the dance, occurs in Chapter 18. Gerald and Gudrun together take a rabbit from its hutch so that it can be sketched. The rabbit struggles violently, lacerating the arms of both of them, and the final "unearthly abhorrent scream" emitted by the rabbit seems to tear "the veil of Gudrun's consciousness" making her "almost unearthly" too. The experience is almost an initiation into obscene mysteries, the blood drawn by the rabbit being a parody of the *Blutbrüderschaft* between Gerald and Birkin. The man and the woman are united in a kind of sophisticated sadism, ironically tinged by the childish imitation of maternal affection with which Gerald's little sister, Winifred, treats the rabbit:

There was a queer, faint, obscene smile over his face. She looked at him and saw him, and knew that he was initiate as she was initiate. This thwarted her, and contravened her, for the moment.

'God be praised we aren't rabbits,' she said, in a high, shrill voice.

The smile intensified a little, on his face.

'Not rabbits?' he said, looking at her fixedly.

Slowly her face relaxed into a smile of obscene recognition.

'Ah Gerald,' she said, in a strong, slow, almost manlike way. '—All that, and more.' Her eyes looked up at him with shocking nonchalance.

He felt again as if she had hit him across the face—or rather, as if she had torn him across the breast, dully, finally. He turned aside.

'Eat, eat my darling!' Winifred was softly conjuring the rabbit, and creeping forward to touch it. It hobbled away from her. 'Let its mother stroke its fur then, darling, because it is so mysterious—.' (Chap. 18)

VI *The Tragedy of Gerald and Gudrun*

Gudrun shares this obscene initiation with Gerald, but not, finally, on equal terms. She gains ascendancy over him. The statement, "He felt again as if she had hit him across the face," refers back to the Highland cattle episode, at the end of which Gerald had appeared, to protect Gudrun, but only to receive a blow upon the cheek, instead. "You have struck the first blow," says Gerald, and Gudrun retorts, "And I shall strike the last"— which is so. In their relationship Gudrun is nearly always fighting from a position of strength. The "free proud singleness" which is the crux of Birkin's idea of marriage is strikingly absent from the Gerald-Gudrun relationship, despite Gerald's "go" and executive toughness. He virtually capitulates to her when, during a spell of prolonged psychic exhaustion that follows his father's death, he creeps into the Brangwen house one night and sleeps with Gudrun. It is not a mutually satisfying love. What Gerald finds in Gudrun is "an infinite relief." He is renewed, but at the cost of sacrificing his independent manhood to the *Magna Mater* figure that Birkin consistently rejects: "And she, she was the great bath of life, he worshipped her. Mother and substance of all life she was. And he, child and man, received of her and was made whole" (Chap. 24).

Their lovemaking brings Gerald "the sleep of complete exhaustion and restoration," but it leaves Gudrun "tormented with violent wakefulness, cast out in the outer darkness." This is not simply an indication of Gerald's failure as a lover. In general he is an efficient Don Juan. But beyond the limits of sheer physical appeal, and the hard will which he displays as an industrial master, he is fatally unsure of himself. It is this weakness which drives him into a desperate seeking of comfort from Gudrun, and which in the end she exploits.

There is one moment when they seem as if they might achieve an equal relationship. This occurs after the Highland cattle episode when Gudrun and Gerald are in the canoe together on the lantern-lit Willey Water. Gudrun "was as if magically aware of their being balanced in separation, in the boat," and the calmness of the night relaxes the tension in Gerald, suggesting a sleep that is quite different from the relief-sleep of his later capitulation to

Gudrun: "His mind was almost submerged, he was almost trans-fused, lapsed out for the first time in his life, into the things about him. For he always kept such a keen attentiveness, concentrated and unyielding in himself. Now he had let go, imperceptibly he was melting into oneness with the whole. It was like pure, perfect sleep, his first great sleep of life" (Chap. 14).

The moment is destroyed, however, by the falling of his sister, Diana, into the water, and the high, piercing shriek of the younger sister, Winifred, which turns Diana's name into a symbol of death: "Di-Di-Di-Di-Oh Di-Oh Di!" Diana's fiancé goes in after her, and Gerald, too, dives into the water in a hopeless attempt at rescue. But he is utterly defeated by the strange underwater world: ". . . when you are down there, it is so cold, actually, and so endless, so different really from what it is on top, so endless—you wonder how it is so many are alive, why we're up here" (Chap. 14).

After the lake had been drained, the bodies of Diana and her fiancé are at last recovered. She had wound her arms so tightly around his neck that she had choked him—a hint of the deadliness of love which foreshadows the change that is to come over the relationship between Gudrun and Gerald. The parallel is not, however, directly between Diana and Gudrun, but between Diana as a member of the ill-fated Crich family and her brother, Gerald. The latter's love for Gudrun is to take on a similarly destructive, clinging quality. And a further significant detail, which colors the whole episode of the water party, is the fact that Gerald's hand has all the time been bandaged, having gotten trapped in some machinery. This hints at the way in which his sacrifice of humanity to the galvanized activity of the industrial entrepreneur cripples him as a lover.

Gudrun's ascendancy is even more apparent in the Austrian mountains. She toys with the idea of marrying Gerald in order to be the impetus behind his great executive ability—"He would be a Napoleon of peace, or a Bismarck—and she the woman behind him"; but the meaninglessness of it all makes her give it up. The fundamental inadequacy of Gerald reveals an inadequacy in Gudrun, too. Her dominance in the relationship can give her no satisfaction. What she wins she does not really want, and she recognizes in the end that this is so. For all her superiority to her lover she also is a tragic figure, for she is dominated herself by destructive powers that make her their instrument, and is equally reduced to a condition of sterile, mechanical monotony. "Oh God," she thinks, "the wheels within wheels of people, it makes one's head tick like a clock, with a very madness of dead mechanical monotony and meaninglessness. How I *hate* life, how I hate it" (Chap. 30). She hates "the Geralds, that they can offer one nothing else," but the bitterness of her situation is that it is only from Gerald (Loerke is no real alternative) that she could hope for anything different. Their fates are intimately bound together. They have the chance to make a marriage. They fail (Lawrence duly recognizes the social forces that contribute to their failure); and, because of this, they are effectually destroyed together.

CHAPTER 5

The Pseudo-Novels:
The Lost Girl,
Aaron's Rod, *and* Kangaroo

THE novels which follow *Women in Love* are of unquestion-
ably inferior quality. Even whether they are true novels at all
is debatable. *The Lost Girl* and *Aaron's Rod* begin convincingly,
but break into two unequal and atmospherically quite different
halves, only too obviously reflecting the circumstances of their
composition. *The Lost Girl* was begun in 1912, broken off owing
to the war, and taken up again in 1920. *Aaron's Rod* was written
partly in 1918 and partly in 1921. *Kangaroo,* written in less than
three months of 1922, bears all the marks of hasty writing with
little revision. The chapter entitled "Bits" is half made up of
brittle anecdotes culled from the pages of the Sydney (Australia)
Bulletin. The Boy in the Bush (1924) is Lawrence's reworking of
a novel by the Australian writer Molly Skinner; and the comic
novel, *Mr. Noon,* which has a certain amount in common with
the first part of *The Lost Girl,* is unfinished.

Diffuseness and casualness mar each of these books. They are
odd mixtures of conventional novel writing, journalism, travel
literature, doctrinal exposition, and satire, illuminated occasionally with those insights into human relationships typical of Lawrence. The artistic wholeness and independent reality of the
great preceding novels has almost vanished. All this must be
frankly recognized. Yet what remains in each book amounts to
more than a fictional miscellany. A kind of unity is provided
by the presence of the author himself—in *Aaron's Rod* and in
Kangaroo he is only very thinly disguised as Lilly and Richard
Lovat Somers, respectively—and though this is harmful to the
novels *as* novels, making it difficult for the reader to enjoy the ex-

perience of an autonomous fictional world, the author's debate with himself gives a wavering, emergent shape to the material.

I The Lost Girl

The Lost Girl is the most rambling and diffuse of Lawrence's novels. Its plot is an extraordinary blend of popular romance and realism. At the beginning of the novel the heroine, Alvina Houghton, is leading a narrow, dispirited life at Woodhouse. Her father, James Houghton, runs a draper's shop—pretentiously, but in such a hopelessly unbusinesslike way that it is ruining the family's fortune. For company Alvina has such aptly named women as Miss Frost, a governess, and Miss Pinnegar, who manages Mr. Houghton's shop and workroom. In an attempt to break out of her dull, parasitic existence Alvina goes to London to train as a midwife, but on returning home she cannot get any patients. She is given new hope, however, when her father has the idea of starting a cinema. His manager, Mr. May, feels the need for some live actors as well as film and so engages a wandering troup called the Natcha-Kee-Tawaras who perform a glamorous Red Indian act. The leader of the troup is a matronly Frenchwoman known as Madame. She plays the part of a squaw, Kishwégin, and the four male members of the troup, including a young Italian named Cicio, take the parts of Indian braves. They act with great panache, forming a vivid, colorful contrast to smoky, gray Woodhouse, and in various odd ways carry over their fictitious characters into their private life.

Alvina falls in love with Cicio, joins the Natcha-Kee-Tawaras as their pianist, and becomes Cicio's mistress. Later she has a revulsion from the sordid traveling actor's life which this involves and becomes deeply suspicious of the pseudo-chivalrous behavior of the "braves" towards Kishwégin. As a result she gives up Cicio. But not for long. For all that he offends her taste and her feminine susceptibilities, Cicio's appeal is mysteriously powerful. When he finds her again, she marries him, and goes with him to his home in the Abruzzi Mountains of Italy. There, instead of the decayed middle-class respectability which she had known in Woodhouse, she has to endure the almost unimaginable poverty of peasant Italy, relieved only by the stark magnificence of the mountain scenery. Alvina finds Pescocalascio (in actuality, Picinisco, described by Lawrence in two remarkable letters of December 16, 1919, and January 9, 1920) dirty and bitterly cold, and her predicament is made worse when Cicio is called to the army, leaving her isolated among foreigners. The novel ends with Cicio's assurance that he will return to her, but there is, in fact, no certainty of this. The very last word spoken by Alvina (in answer to Cicio's "I'll come back") is a question: "Sure?," the ambiguity of which is left unresolved.

A useful clue to the meaning of *The Lost Girl* is to be found in a letter that Lawrence wrote from Italy on October 6, 1912:

> I have read *Anna of the Five Towns* today. . . . to be in Hanley, and to read almost my own dialect, makes me feel quite ill. I hate England and its hopelessness. I hate Bennett's resignation. Tragedy ought really to be a great kick at misery. But *Anna of the Five Towns* seems like an acceptance—so does all the modern stuff since Flaubert. . . . I don't believe England need be so grubby. What does it matter if one is poor, and risks one's livelihood, and reputation. One can have the necessary things, life, and love, and clean warmth. Why is England so shabby?

The Lost Girl is at once an imitation of, and a protest against, the realism of Arnold Bennett. Alvina does not "accept" her Woodhouse existence; she rebels against it. Cicio stands for something not only more romantic, but more real to her. This is not, however, to say that Lawrence quite succeeds in doing what he wants to do with Cicio. The impression created by the novel is that Alvina deceives herself about Cicio, in spite of her awareness of his faults, and one cannot altogether avoid the conclusion that Lawrence himself is struggling to impose upon the reader an image of Cicio which his own novelist's imagination refuses to entertain. What Lawrence offers us as an alternative to Arnold Bennett's realism is not just another version of "escape" literature. This is underlined by the fact that there is no easy transition from the boredom of industrial Woodhouse to some spuriously idealized peasant community in Pescocalascio. Lawrence faces both the physical discomfort that Alvina brings upon herself and her appalling psychological isolation at the end.

The early part of the novel is the part which is most under the influence of Arnold Bennett. Woodhouse is once again Eastwood. Several of the people and episodes, such as the attempt to get a cinema going, are taken from real life. Already, however, Lawrence is losing his inwardness with his native region. He can still sympathetically enjoy the immaculate raffishness of Mr. May and give a detached portrait in Madame of the matriarchal Frenchwoman who is caught between a sentimental romanticism and a shrewd instinct for money and property. Alvina herself is a girl with independence and common sense, and it is entirely consistent with her character that she should tackle the harsh life of a midwife delivering babies in the London slums rather than relapse into the same sort of existence as Miss Frost. But the interesting and attractive characters tend to be those who are not in or of Woodhouse. Excellent though Lawrence's realism is, it is biased. It is not the objective realism of Bennett, which to Lawrence is "like an acceptance," but a "kick" against the suffocating dullness and moral constriction of Woodhouse. And running through the novel, intermittently, and patchily realized, is the countervailing experience of a more vigorous way of life.

A connection can also be made with *The Trespasser,* in that the harshness of the realism offsets a rather oddly romantic streak —though here it would be more accurate to say that the latter is an attempt to offset the former. This romanticism is chiefly associated with the Natcha-Kee-Tawaras. To begin with, their play-acting is very much in the spirit of the Palermo marionettes described at the end of *Sea and Sardinia.* The procession through the streets of Woodhouse—Kishwégin in her deerskin riding a white horse, the men in war paint and feathers and "brilliant Navajo blankets," and Cicio "extraordinarily velvety and alive on horseback"—does have a gay, exciting freshness that forms a startling contrast to the "grey and heavy" colliers. But, when Lawrence attempts to make something deeper out of the Natcha-Kee-Tawaras, the result is embarrassing. The worst element comes out in his writing, which is peppered with such phrases as "dark, mysterious glamour" and "the ragged chant of strong male voices, resonant and gay with mockery." Their elaborate rituals and the "ceremony" of Alvina's initiation into the mysteries of the Natcha-Kee-Tawaras are treated half-humorously, half-seriously—Lawrence seems not to want to clear away the ambiguity.

Most disastrous of all is Alvina's relationship with Cicio which is a painfully banal example of the competent "white" woman succumbing to the "dark" potent male. In this part of the novel Lawrence descends to the level of the cheap novelette. Alvina's experience foreshadows that of Kate in *The Plumed Serpent,* with Cicio the forerunner of Don Cipriano. There is something willful in Lawrence's forcing her into the embrace of Cicio; it is quite out of keeping with the character she is given in the book as a whole. The general contrast between the sharply distinct maleness of Cicio and the effeminacy of characters like James Houghton and Mr. May is effective enough, but the quality of Lawrence's writing fails to make the particular affair between Alvina and Cicio convincing.

Lawrence does not, however, pretend that Cicio is a glamorous being, other than as a dark, "sensual" lover. Like Hadrian in the story, "You Touched Me," he has a hard head for money. Alvina feels that he subtly insults her: "Cicio would have had a lifelong respect for her, if she had come with even so paltry a sum as two hundred pounds. Now she had nothing, he would coolly withhold this respect. She felt he might jeer at her" (Chap. 10). The sordid peasant reality of Pescocalascio is embodied in him, and Alvina is not allowed to be blind to it. Money is very much an obsession of Woodhouse, too, and Lawrence is perhaps trying to distinguish between money as an end in itself and money as a necessary means. Yet, coupled as it is with the gross peasant mentality of Cicio, it gives the rather different impression that Lawrence intends to tie his romantic antithesis of Woodhouse to a realism as exacting as but more penetrating than Bennett's. This intention is not realized at the very point where it most needs convincing realization—in the presentation of the mystical brotherhood and son-mother relationship of the Natcha-Kee-Tawaras and in the treatment of the love of Alvina and Cicio— but it makes *The Lost Girl* an interesting failure. One can see Lawrence tussling with his own impatience with realism and putting it to the test of, admittedly very imperfect, art.

II   Aaron's Rod

F. R. Leavis notes the "spirit of unembarrassed tentativeness" [1] in which *Aaron's Rod* is written. In this novel hectoringly repetitive assertions, of a kind rather too frequent in Lawrence's doctrinal works, are made as if with *ex cathedra* authority, but their positiveness is only a disguise for a probing uncertainty. "Tentativeness" of this sort implies the leaving of a good many loose ends, and there is no denying that *Aaron's Rod* is the most formless and disconnected of Lawrence's novels. Some sort of unifying theme (apart from the rough-and-ready unity provided by the threading of a number of disparate episodes on the string of

Aaron Sisson's experience) can be found, however, in the dislike of "bullying," particularly as it affects love and marriage.

The subjection of husband to the interests of his wife and family seems to be the cause of Aaron's abandoning his home and traveling abroad to see what the world has to offer him. The opening section, which shows the end of Aaron's marriage, and Chapter 9, in which Aaron pays a return visit to his wife, thinking that they might possibly be able to start again, are the parts most recognizably belonging to a novel. In these the stalemate of the marriage is not so much talked about as presented. Aaron's wife is a nagging woman. She instinctively sides with her children against her husband, even when the children are merely possessive and willful, as Millicent is when she breaks one of the glass decorations for her Christmas tree. On the other hand, Aaron is not a very attractive husband. He does, as his wife asserts, take "unfair advantage" when he uses his masculine freedom to go off to the public house, while she must stay at home to look after the children; and his rather coolly ironic attitude towards his children suggests a lack of responsibility and of natural human feeling. The flute (Aaron's "rod"), which he plays to console himself, also suggests a willingness to escape from the situation he has got himself into, rather than face it; and this tendency is confirmed by his desertion. Later on Aaron meets Lilly, a man who, like Birkin in *Women in Love*, is very much a spokesman for Lawrence's own ideas, and it is Lilly who helps him to see the breakdown of his domestic life as a symptom of the general disease afflicting modern marriage: ". . . marriage wants readjusting—or extending—to get men on to their own legs once more, and to give them the adventure again. But men won't stick together and fight for it. Because once a woman has climbed up with her children, she'll find plenty of grovellers ready to support her and suffocate any defiant spirit. And women will sacrifice eleven men, fathers, husbands, brothers and lovers, for one baby —or for her own female self-conceit" (Chap. 9).

But this is not an altogether satisfactory explanation of what has actually been presented in the opening part of the novel. Aaron is in a sense bullied by his wife, but it is clear that he bullies, or exploits, his masculine privileges, too. The relationship between them has never reached maturity, and the one justification for Aaron's abandoning his family (Lawrence, it is obvious from the novel, felt the need for justifying it) is that it may be a way of opening up new experience to him which will possibly complete the growth of their relationship.

Once away from the mining area of Aaron's home, the novel-like quality declines. The depiction of the Bohemian set into whose company Aaron falls is thin and unconvincing. Jim Bricknell is a caricature of the male who is quite incapable of independence. His clamoring to be loved is a crude exaggeration of the Christian ideal of love, allied with adoration of the female, which is so wordily denounced by Lilly. (Jim is quite often literally unable to get on his "own legs once more.") Hovering on the edge of this set, half of it, and half despising it, is Lilly himself, under whose influence Aaron now comes. It is a common criticism that there are times when Lilly and Aaron are indistinguishable. Both tend to become media for the views and experiences of their creator. But in general the intention seems to be to present Aaron as the sensitive, unusual, but relatively inarticulate working man and Lilly as the educated, conscious opponent of the established order who is able to voice and interpret Aaron's instinctive rejection of that order. The crudeness and superficiality of much of Lilly's thought prompt the remark that Lilly's guiding of Aaron is too much like the blind leading the blind. If it were not for Lilly's wife, Tanny (transparently Frieda), who gives her husband some of those valuable "digs in the ribs" prescribed in *Fantasia of the Unconscious*,[2] Lilly would appear an insufferably self-opinionated bore.

Women in Love had ended with Birkin's saying that relationship with a woman was not enough. He wanted "eternal union with a man too: another kind of love." The possibilities of this were explored in the proposed *Blutbrüderschaft* between Gerald and Birkin. An attempt at reviving and extending this is made in the friendship between Lilly and Aaron, but the relationship is that of master and disciple, rather than of equals. The episode in which Aaron falls sick and is nursed by Lilly roughly corresponds to the "Gladiatorial" chapter of *Women in Love* (in which Gerald and Birkin wrestle together). A similar physical intimacy is established by Lilly's rubbing Aaron with oil: "For a long time he rubbed finely and steadily, then went over the whole of the lower body, mindless, as if in a sort of incantation. He rubbed every speck of the man's lower body—the abdomen, the buttocks, the thighs and knees, down to the feet, rubbed it all warm and glowing with camphorated oil, every bit of it, chafing the toes swiftly, till he was almost exhausted" (Chap. 9).

This passage inevitably raises the question of homosexuality. It has been said that Aaron and Lilly "are looking for a substitute for marriage rather than a solution of its problems," [3] and various critics have suspected Lawrence of a leaning towards sexual perversion. This view seems doubtful because of the central importance he gives to marriage and "polarity." A more feasible explanation is suggested by the exploratory impetus behind *Aaron's Rod*. Concerned, as he always is, with wholeness, Lawrence insists on finding a place for the physical as well as the intellectual and emotional in human relationships. This works well enough between man and woman, but where a man-man relationship is concerned it meets with the resistance of a taboo so strong that the physical cannot be introduced without causing profound unease.

The experimental *Blutbrüderschaft* of Aaron and Lilly does not last, however. Lilly insists that he will only have friends who are in fundamental agreement with him. After a visit by a war hero, Herbertson, who is shattered by his experiences and must go around, like the Ancient Mariner, unloading them on any audience he can find, Lilly and Aaron get involved in an argument about the reality of the war. To Lilly it was all false, made possible by the acquiescence of men in a condition of "mob-sleep." Poison gas is the evidence of this. But Aaron remarks, "It's the wide-awake ones that invent the poison gas, and use it. Where should we be without it?" Somewhat melodramatically Lilly makes this an issue on which their whole friendship depends; and, since Aaron will not retract, Lilly orders him out of his flat. (It is one among several indications of the carelessness with which this book is written that when they meet again in Italy the issue, which was considered vital enough to be a test of the friendship, is forgotten.) As Aaron says, "Everybody's got to agree with you—that's your price." The episode brings out sharply the master-disciple aspect of the relationship, and shows how impossible it is. Yet Lilly returns to it at the end of the novel when he tells Aaron that he must submit himself to "a more heroic soul." "And whom shall I submit to?" asks Aaron. To which Lilly makes the not so very enigmatic reply, "Your soul will tell you." If Lilly were a properly objectified character, one could only regard this as comedy underlining his inability to learn from experience, but because of his obvious closeness to Lawrence himself it can only be regarded as evidence of the pertinacity with which Lawrence sometimes clings to an idea, even when it has been thoroughly tested by his imagination and found wanting.

It is all too easy to find fault with *Aaron's Rod*. The novel is not only shoddily constructed, and in many places shoddily written, but it is frequently absurd in a way that lays it open to those critics who take pleasure in sniping at Lawrence. Yet the book has very readable passages, even after the opening, which is so decidedly superior to the rest. The chapters dealing with Aaron's weekend at the Italian home of Sir William Franks are lively social satire, as are the episodes dealing with the two young, upper-middle-class dilettantes, Angus and Francis, and with the English colony in Florence. These parts of the novel tend to become gossipy, *roman à clef* material, which loses its sparkle as the once topical personalities begin to share the obscurity of their eighteenth-century equivalents in Pope's *Dunciad*, but they still survive as amusing comic sketches. The glimpses of Turin, Milan, the Lombardy plain, and Florence remind one of Lawrence's gift for capturing the spirit of place, evident in the travel books and in the letters. In these passages the novel takes on the quality of a vivid, impressionistic diary. When the slipshod harangues of Lilly are forgotten, one still remembers the brilliant, alert descriptions of the young Italian Socialist climbing up the side of a house in Milan to tear down the Italian national flag, and then climbing painfully and ignominiously down to be arrested by the Carabinieri.

III Kangaroo

Much of *Kangaroo*[4] is argumentative and seemingly didactic, but the didacticism is more apparent than real. Lawrence's reasoning is essentially a rationalization of his intuitions, and the action and personages of the novel are an extension of this process into plot structure and character. The result is something akin to a Morality play dealing with the conflicting demands of authority and individualism but with this important difference: there is no fixed, predetermined body of doctrine for the novel to dramatize.

Kangaroo is also a proving ground for the problems that faced Lawrence personally after 1918. (The protagonist, Richard

Lovat Somers, is once again remarkably like Lawrence himself, and his wife, Harriet, is very much a fictional portrait of Frieda.) The most obviously personal thing in the novel is the chapter entitled "The Nightmare," which deals with Lawrence's own experience in Cornwall during the war. This is not thrust irrelevantly into the middle of the book, for it provides an explanation of what drives Somers away from England and brings him to Australia. The cause lies in Somers' resentment at the treatment he received from the authorities during the war and at being ordered to leave his cottage on the Cornish coast. His individuality and integrity seem to him to have been abused by crass officials who embody wartime England's hysterical fear of anyone or anything that will not fit into the crude, jingoistic pattern of the time.

After the war Somers and Harriet leave England as quickly as they can; and, as they look back from their boat at the snow-covered cliffs of Kent, "England looked like a grey, dreary-grey coffin sinking in the sea behind." This does not quite carry the weight of conviction that Lawrence intends. He seems to be giving vent to a mood rather than seeing with the eyes of the imagination. In this respect the passage is symptomatic of the "Nightmare" chapter as a whole. Although the theme fully justifies Lawrence's seriousness of purpose, the element of personal injury seems to be magnified by a mind throwing itself unreservedly into the sensation of the moment and failing to make the attempt at an adult assessment of its pain. The experience embodied in the chapter is not fully worked out. Consequently, when Somers abandons England he is not so completely turning his back on the past as he imagines. England has thrown up the problem of authority and the individual, and this is a problem that he cannot evade by simply leaving the country. Nor can he escape the influence of his homeland. It has left its mark in the very sensitivity that makes him react as he does to officialdom, and it will make him equally disgusted with the opposite extreme of anarchy.

Nothing shows this more clearly than the Englishness of Somers' reactions to Australia. In *The Boy in the Bush* and in *Kangaroo* Australia is present as a land of "freedom." None of the tension and restraint of the Old World exists there. In Sydney, life goes on casually, amicably, and without any obvious pressure of authority: it is a city of "democracy." Yet these Lawrentian alter egos who come to Australia from England do not fit in with this democratic mode. Jack, the hero of *The Boy in the Bush*, is intensely and self-consciously English, despite the fact that he has been virtually exiled to Australia for his wildness and refusal to be tamed. He is a great social success in the congenial atmosphere of "free" Australia, but he keeps essentially aloof, quietly insisting on his individuality and superiority. Somers, in *Kangaroo*, is not even so sociable as Jack, though every bit as aloof and English. To the workmen lounging in Macquarie Street he is a "foreign-looking little stranger," and when he speaks it is in "unmistakeable English: English of the old country."

The purpose of the first chapter is to establish this Australia-England antithesis. The ease and the lack of tension of the Australians are sympathetically presented, but qualified by the crudeness of their responses and their slang. Harriet and Somers appear at first unsympathetic aliens keeping themselves coldly apart, but they are also felt to have the reticence of more introspective natures. As the chapter proceeds, Australia is seen more restrictively through the eyes of the newcomers, but with the qualifications implied by the manner in which they are presented at the beginning. To them the Australian slackness is near-chaos. Their reactions are dramatically conceived, but they also enable Lawrence to suggest how "freedom" must look against the traditionalist assumptions of the European. Somers complains of the taxi driver who overcharges him. The bungalows of Murdoch Street are ranged "dot-dot-dot, close together and yet apart, like modern democracy." The Australians seem "uncouth," their familiarity "aggressive." Their very classlessness is damning, for "Somers was English by blood and education . . . he felt himself to be one of the *responsible* members of society. . . . In old, cultured, ethical England this distinction is radical between the responsible members of society and the irresponsible" (Chap. 1). In Australia, "Demos" is "his own master, undisputed." The country appears to be running smoothly, but perhaps it is "a machine running on but gradually running down."

Australian freedom is thus at once attractive and repulsive to Somers. It is a natural preparation for his encounter with his Australian neighbor, Jack Callcott, and his consequent introduction to the Digger movement which is led by Ben Cooley ("Kangaroo"). The movement's hierarchical structure corresponds politically to Somers' distinction between "the responsible members

of society and the irresponsible." Indeed its organization and the
ideal on which it is based would seem more European than Australian. But it also has a genuinely Australian character. The
shortness of Lawrence's stay in Australia suggests that he had
little opportunity to learn about the country's politics; but, apart
from his remarkable intuitive gift that always has to be reckoned
with, Lawrence learned a great deal from the Sydney *Bulletin*.[5]

The Digger movement is divided within itself. The paramilitary
organization and contempt for "vote-catching" form an uneasy
alliance with the doctrines of mateship and absolute love, and
this is reflected in the characters of Jack Callcott and Kangaroo
himself. Kangaroo is trying to create a political movement out of
the union of authority and absolute love, but Harriet rightly
divines the basis of Jack's membership when she says, "He's a
returned war hero, and he wants a chance of keeping on being a
hero." His idea of authority is, fundamentally, the same as that
unquestioning obedience which Somers came up against so bitterly in wartime England; and it is a consummate piece of irony
that, in the first stage of intimacy with Jack, Somers should de-
ceive himself into thinking that he is encountering "a new feeling." Disillusionment inevitably follows, when in a political brawl
Jack shows that he has the brutal instincts of a stormtrooper.
The scene is prophetic of Nazism, but should be conclusive
evidence that Lawrence's sympathies did not lie in that direction.
Jack is shown as degraded to an inhuman level:

'I got one of them iron bars from the windows, and I stirred the brains
of a couple of them with it, and I broke the neck of a third. . . .
Cripes, there's *nothing* bucks you up sometimes like killing a man—
nothing. . . . When it comes over you, you know, there's nothing else
like it. *I* never knew, till the war. And I wouldn't believe it then, not
for many a while. But it's *there*. Cripes, it's there right enough. Having
a woman's something, isn't it? But it's a flea-bite, nothing, compared to
killing your man when your blood comes up.' (Chap. 16)

The crude, impoverished language, the explicit connection with
the war, and the self-damning comparison with the sexual act are
too obvious in implication to need further comment.

Kangaroo himself had wanted to avoid violence of this sort, but
his tragedy is that he never realizes the extent to which he bears
responsibility for the riot and the degradation that it reveals.
The brutality in Jack is also an unacknowledged part of his own

nature. A hint of this had been conveyed in the critical interview between Somers and Kangaroo in Chapter 11 where Somers admits his lack of faith in the doctrine of absolute love. Frustrated in his attempt to win over Somers, Kangaroo is momentarily transformed into "a thing, not a whole man," and Somers has a sudden fear that Kangaroo will assault him. The latent violence of this scene and the actual violence of the brawl are linked by Kangaroo's refusal to acknowledge claims that lie outside the ideal of absolute love. Because of his blindness to the contradictions in the Digger movement, a streak of savagery is allowed to develop until it is too late to check it. Kangaroo tries to exalt the spirit above the body, and it is Lawrentian retributive justice that he receives a wound in his stomach which turns his own body into something vile and sickly smelling. The political and the personal catastrophes are thus brought together, demonstrating the inadequacy of an ideal that ignores the "whole man."

The sea and the bush dominate the last thirty pages of the novel. Both, of course, are present throughout; but, until the collapse of the Digger movement, their function is simply to be a reminder of the immense natural forces which provide the context of human life. This is made explicit in Chapter 9, "Harriet and Lovat at Sea in Marriage," where the age-old images of the sea and the ship of life are used to express the conflict between Somers and his wife for the "maistrie." But in the latter part of the novel the sea and the bush become important enough to dwarf the characters instead of serving as a mere background. After the death of Kangaroo, Somers turns to the sea for relief from the disgust that involvement with the Diggers has inspired in him; and he finds it in an expression of "the mystery of apartness." The descriptions of the seascape and sea life which follow contain some of the best writing in *Kangaroo;* the words flicker with life in the peculiarly Lawrentian fashion and the whole is executed by an imagination that can enter with exceptional intensity into the nonhuman world.

Emphasis on the sea culminates in the storm which isolates Harriet and Somers, forcing withdrawal from the world upon them and symbolizing their dedication to "the mystery of apartness." When the storm abates everything seems to have been swept clean, and there follows a lyrically pure Australian spring which is the symbol of a renewal of life. It gives Harriet and Somers an entirely new love for Australia, but this love has no effect now on their determination to leave for America. There is no suggestion that America is a land of hope to which the renewal naturally points. In fact, the decision to leave or to stay seems to matter only at the story level and to have no further significance. What does matter is that life is freed from the grip of a false authority that would suffocate it in the name of benevolent idealism and that it asserts itself more vigorously and profusely than before, though with "a stillness, and a manlessness."

CHAPTER 6

The Late Novels:
The Plumed Serpent *and*
Lady Chatterley's Lover

IN *Women in Love* Lawrence offers the marriage of Birkin and
Ursula as an alternative to the industrialized and will-domi-
nated civilization that he detests, but already the *Blutbrüderschaft* of Birkin and Gerald suggests a dissatisfaction with an alternative that is limited to the relationship between a man and a
woman. *Aaron's Rod* carries this dissatisfaction further, and in
Kangaroo Lawrence experiments with a wider political alternative. This is a failure, and Somers turns away to the dark gods as
implicit in the Australian bush. It was a logical next step for Lawrence to attempt in *The Plumed Serpent* the imagination of an
alternative based directly on the dark gods themselves.

The result is not a failure of exactly the same kind as in *Kangaroo,* but the novel leaves the reader very uneasy and seems (in
spite of the statement, "I consider this my most important novel,
so far"[1]) to have come out of Lawrence's head rather than his
true novelist's imagination. The relationship of Kate, the heroine
of *The Plumed Serpent,* to the Quetzalcoatl cult, and to the Mexican general, Don Cipriano, in particular, suggests a conflict between the individual and the larger corporate ideal which is still
unresolved. Kate is an Irishwoman. Her first husband had di-
vorced her ten years ago, and her second husband is dead. She is
now at the difficult age of forty, disillusioned with her previous
life and with European ideals in particular. The descendant of
Ursula and Gudrun, and of Tanny and Harriet (and with a
strong likeness, once more, to Lawrence's own wife, Frieda),
Kate represents an independent type of woman who commanded

profound respect from Lawrence, but of whom he was also profoundly critical. By the end of *The Plumed Serpent* one can see that his need to come to terms with Kate has a much greater hold on his imagination than the Quetzalcoatl cult. He is confronted again with the basic sexual problem of *Women in Love*, and in his next and final novel, *Lady Chatterley's Lover*, it is this problem which once more becomes the central theme; the social implications, though not discarded, are relegated to the background.

I The Plumed Serpent: *The Religion of Quetzalcoatl*

A great impetus was given to Lawrence's attempt at direct presentation of the dark gods by his coming to America in 1922, the implications of which have already been mentioned in comments about *Mornings in Mexico* and about the other American essays (see Introduction, p. 26). The fundamental difficulty that he had to face in attempting a fictional realization of the old animistic religion of the Indians was that it was, as Lawrence himself says, a "religion which precedes the god-concept, and is therefore greater and deeper than any god-religion." [2] He therefore chose the ancient Aztec religion of Mexico, which was a "god-religion," but which was steeped in cruelty and meanness. The sadism of the Aztecs is fully recognized in the essay from *Mornings in Mexico* called "The Mozo," but in *The Plumed Serpent*, although Lawrence does not ignore it, he falls into a terrible moral confusion about it. What we have in the novel, consequently, is a strange mixture of a genuinely moving religious inspiration, which derives from Lawrence's sympathy with the Indians of New Mexico, and a spurious sadistic cult deriving from his peculiar adaptation of the Aztec pantheon.

Don Ramón, a Mexican landowner, is the leader of the new Quetzalcoatl, or "Plumed Serpent," cult which springs up on the shores of Lake Sayula. His chief lieutenant in this enterprise is Don Cipriano. Ramón's aim is to revive the ancient, indigenous religion of America—in the words of Kate, who is attracted by the idea, to "take up the old, broken impulse that will connect us with the mystery of the cosmos again." But since the people can only have immediate, passional knowledge through symbols and myths, Ramón feels it necessary to embody this religion in the personal gods and ritual of the Aztecs. Ramón himself takes the part of the god Quetzalcoatl; Don Cipriano figures as the militant Huitzilopochtli; and Kate, somewhat reluctantly, agrees to appear as the goddess Malintzi.

Ramón draws his strength not from playacting the part of Quetzalcoatl—this exhausts him—but from a trancelike condition in which he reaches: "pure unconsciousness, neither hearing nor feeling nor knowing, like a dark sea-weed deep in the sea. With no Time and no World, in the deeps that are timeless and worldless" (Chap. 13). In the cyclic myth which he constructs of the weary Jesus and the Madonna withdrawing from Mexico to the place behind the sun, and of Quetzalcoatl returning as a rejuvenated god, the "religion which precedes the god-concept" is implicit. Quetzalcoatl and Jesus are but "manifestations"—the word used by Ramón, and stressed several times—of the primitive, animistic force. The point is sufficiently underlined in various places, as when Ramón says to his first wife, Carlota, that "Quetzalcoatl is just a living word, for these people, no more." Or when he answers his son's objection that "There never was any Quetzalcoatl, except idols" with the question, "Is there any Jesus, except images?"

The main objection to the Quetzalcoatl cult is that it debases the central religious experience. To those who regard Lawrence as "spiritually sick," such debasement will seem merely the realization of what is already implicit in that experience; but, as far as the present writer is concerned, the health of the fundamental impulses in the book is not in doubt. What is disturbing about the cult is that, as Lawrence builds up its ritual and progress, he seems to fall into the very mood of violence and cruelty which has been rejected at the beginning of the novel, especially by Kate, as a condition of decadence. The religion of Quetzalcoatl should be the antithesis of the bullfight described in the first chapter, with its nauseating disemboweling of two old horses and the effeminate toreadors. Kate is supposed to regain the "fear tempered with reverence of the great Mithraic beast" which the stupidity of the bulls in the ring had caused her to lose. Ramón does proclaim a return to the radical distinctness of the sexes which counters the decadent effeminacy of the toreadors, and it is possible to see his encouraging the peons to take a new pride in themselves as an antidote to the mob spirit of the spectators at the bullfight. But the ritual in which Cipriano's guards break the necks of two prisoners, and Cipriano himself, tricked out in war paint and feathers, stabs three others, is far more disgusting than anything in the bullfight. Lawrence calls this act an "execution," but it is obviously inspired by the human sacrifices of the Aztecs.

One possible effect of this episode could have been to show the betrayal of the religious revolution. Ramón is once or twice uneasy about the fate of his venture. He expects betrayal and even feels that Cipriano may relapse from a faithful disciple into an ambitious Mexican general. Cipriano is, in fact, a slightly doubtful ally. He would like to turn the movement into a political *putsch,* and it seems that he gets at last some of his way, for we are told rather perfunctorily by Lawrence that the new religion eventually displaces Catholicism and is installed by President Montes as the official Mexican religion. Yet it is clearly not intended by Lawrence that the new movement should be seen as collapsing into the decadence from which it was originally meant to rescue Mexico. He in some way loses contact with his original purpose so that the reinvigorating animism of the Indians gives way to the cruelty of the Aztecs.

II The Plumed Serpent: *Kate*

Kate's reaction to the "execution" is significant. For a woman of her common sense and humane feelings, her response is surprisingly mild:

> The executions shocked and depressed her. She knew that Ramón and Cipriano did deliberately what they did: they believed in their deeds, they acted with all their conscience. And as men, probably they were right.
> But they seemed nothing but men. When Cipriano said: *Man that is man is more than a man,* he seemed to be driving the male significance to its utmost, and beyond, with a sort of demonism. It seemed to her all terrible *will,* the exertion of pure, awful will.   (Chap. 24)

But she is also fascinated and "spellbound," though "not utterly acquiescent. In one corner of her soul, was revulsion and a touch of nausea." Lawrence himself, here, is obviously not quite sure what to say. Kate's rather weak criticism of Ramón and Cipriano indicates how far her old values have been exchanged for the new ones of the Quetzalcoatl cult, and the spell under which she falls is, in relation to her general development in the novel, supposedly a sign of grace. But her criticism also provides an outlet for Lawrence's own instinctive revulsion; and, from that point of view, the muted quality of her reaction is felt, not as the lingering on of an old way of feeling which must be superseded, but as the willfulness of the author smothering his own doubts. The "exertion of pure, awful will" is, in the end, Lawrence's own; and it perhaps provides a clue to what goes wrong in his presentation of the Quetzalcoatl religion.

Kate's position in the novel is crucial. Through her, the new religion is related to the old, spiritually overdeveloped consciousness of European civilization. Lawrence's intention with regard to her is roughly the same as with the woman of "The Woman Who Rode Away," and can be stated more clearly, because it is expressed in a more baldly simplified way, in the words of that tale: "Her kind of womanhood, intensely personal and individual, was to be obliterated again, and the great primeval symbols were to tower once more over the fallen individual independence of woman. The sharpness and the quivering nervous consciousness of the highly-bred white woman was to be destroyed again, womanhood was to be cast once more into the great stream of impersonal sex and impersonal passion."

Kate is, however, a fully developed "character" in a way that the woman of the tale cannot be, and this development involves a more subtle presentation of her thoughts and feelings. She is a living human being facing the problems of the two ways of life, not simply a symbol of white womanhood. This position makes her a very interesting person, and the parts of the novel which relate her individual experiences are far superior to the rest. (As Graham Hough says, "Everything seen through the eyes of Kate is adequate and realized."[3]) But her very reality as a woman plays havoc with Lawrence's doctrinal intention. The honesty with which he presents Kate makes it impossible for him to pretend that such a woman as she is would wholly and without very serious reservations accept the religion of Quetzalcoatl and the kind of love that Don Cipriano offers her.

Jascha Kessler has suggested that the true myth embodied in *The Plumed Serpent* is not that of the risen Quetzalcoatl, but the pattern of "separation-initiation-return" in terms of which primitive societies met certain of the fundamental problems of life.[4] Lawrence is unlikely to have consciously had such a pattern in mind, but it is nevertheless a useful suggestion for the interpretation of Kate's personal history. The first part of the novel deals largely with her dissatisfaction as a "highly-bred white woman," both with her own European background and the half-Americanized, half-savage decadence of Mexico City. Her journey to Lake Sayula, which is the finest passage of writing in the novel, is her "separation" from this declining way of life and also a transition to the new world of Quetzalcoatl into which she is later to be "initiated." (The last part of the formula, "return," does not apply to *The Plumed Serpent,* but it is, according to Kessler, embodied in "The Escaped Cock.")

Lawrence uses a number of symbolic and imagistic details to link the earlier part of the novel with the later predominantly Quetzalcoatl part. References, for example, to the snake, or the Aztec dragon, and to the morning star anticipate the formal symbolism of the Quetzalcoatl insignia. But it is in the description of Kate's journey that Lawrence most successfully suggests a transformation of the "spirit of place" appropriate to a new, revelatory experience. The water of Lake Sayula becomes "sperm-like" and "earth-filmy, hardly water at all. The lymphatic milk of fishes." Kate finds calm and dignity in the peasants who help her on her journey (they turn out to be Quetzalcoatl's men) and serenity in the atmosphere. Lawrence changes his style, too, in keeping with this mood—it acquires something of the incantatory quality of the poetry—and Kate finds herself using slightly odd phrases like "the Great Breath."[5] (This suggests the similar phrasing and rather similar journey of Gethin Day in the unfinished novel, *The Flying Fish.*) The transition is thus accompanied by a shift from the prosaic to the poetic use of language which leads naturally enough to the chants and hymns of Quetzalcoatl—though the latter use unfortunately suggests that Don Ramón, whatever his distinction as a religious leader, is a thoroughly bad poet.

At Sayula, Kate sets up house and acquires a few Mexican servants whose life is freshly and realistically described. The novel once again becomes recognizably a novel. Kate herself enters a long phase of attraction towards, and repulsion from, the Quetzalcoatl cult which shows Lawrence's great gift for rendering the fluctuating, indirect movement of a woman's sympathies, and further strengthens the book as a true, novel-like record of human experience. She allows herself, somewhat reluctantly, to be drawn into the cult as the living representative of the goddess Malintzi, the counterpoise and mate of Cipriano who is "the living Huitzilopochtli"—a decision which, again, strains credibility. What is real, however, is Lawrence's exploration of the love relationship between Kate and Cipriano, and it becomes the dominant theme of the last three chapters.

In these chapters, which form a sort of coda to the novel as a whole, a completely new character is introduced in the shape of Teresa, the woman who becomes Ramón's wife after the death of the fanatically devout Carlota. Teresa is intended as a corrective to Kate. She does not value her independence and self-sufficiency. When her husband is exhausted, she abandons herself entirely to the task of giving him rest; and—though Lawrence does not say so explicitly—she accepts it as her function to be the uncritical adorer and supporter of her husband. Kate is naturally slightly contemptuous of Teresa for taking this attitude, but it is she, not Teresa, whom Lawrence would have the reader regard as misguided. Teresa is the womanly woman whose relationship with Ramón is supposedly a telling contrast with Kate's inability to lose her assertive individuality and so find real satisfaction in her relationship with Cipriano.

The connection between Kate and Cipriano is of a peculiar kind. It resembles the impersonal "polarity" that Birkin preaches to Ursula, but it is stripped of all that is recognizably warm and human. That Kate should have consented to be "married" to Cipriano within the Quetzalcoatl cult is difficult enough to believe, but that she should also agree to a civil marriage and to living with him in the normal way only serves to emphasize the abnormality and implausibility of their relationship. Cipriano refuses to give her satisfaction when they make love—something which her second husband, Joachim, had always given her. Lawrence implies that this, too, is a part of her false European values that Kate must surrender. She does, apparently, learn "the worthlessness of this foam-effervescence"; and, in place of the old hyperconscious way of life, she comes to accept passivity and unconsciousness. Cipriano will allow her no personal knowledge of him at all;

And as it was in the love-act, so it was with him. She could not *know* him. When she tried to know him, something went slack in her, and she had to leave off. She had to let be. She had to leave him, dark and hot and potent, along with the things that *are*, but are not known. The presence. And the stranger. This he was always to her.

There was hardly anything to say to him. And there was no personal intimacy. He kept his privacy round him like a cloak, and left her immune within her own privacy. He was a stranger to her, she to him. (Chap. 26)

By any normal standards this is no marriage at all. The chapter from which this comes is entitled "Kate Is a Wife," but the statement is almost meaningless. Cipriano is even less a "husband." At the best he is a poetic symbol. The novel is once again forced to the level of poetic rather than of realistic expression. In trying to reveal what Kate does find in Cipriano, Lawrence virtually uses the same material as in his poems. The description for example, of Cipriano's wading out into the sun-reddened water is a prose counterpart of the poem, "For the Heroes are dipped in Scarlet." And the snake which Kate watches retreating into a hole, at the very end of this chapter, is a close analogue to the snake of Lawrence's most celebrated poem. Kate's ability to accept Cipriano is beautifully created on this poetic level. But he is incredible as an actual partner for whose sake Kate is willing to abandon all her old notions of freedom and independence. This is tacitly acknowledged in the ambiguity of the last words of the novel: "You won't let me go!" This statement is both an admission of the powerful hold that Cipriano's "sensuality" has over Kate and a reservation of her right to disagree with and deny him.

III Lady Chatterley's Lover: *Characteristics of the Third Version*

One of the delicate minor incidents in *Lady Chatterley's Lover* is that in which Mellors gives Connie a chick to hold: "She took the little drab thing between her hands, and there it stood, on its impossible little stalk of legs, its atom of balancing life trembling through its almost weightless feet into Connie's hands. But it lifted its handsome, clean-shaped little head boldly, and looked sharply round, and gave a little 'peep'" (Chap. 10).

This incident recalls with a significant difference, the episode in which Kate rescues a chick from a Mexican boy who has been throwing stones at it, only to see it retrieved by the boy's older brother and submitted to the stoning game again. She reflects that to the boy the chick is merely an alien creature; he is blind to it as a "soft struggling thing finding its own fluttering way through life." The boy's cruelty seems to be condoned, and Kate's very natural and humane act of compassion is not only ineffectual (she does not attempt a second rescue), but also made to appear slightly effete, as though the relic of an outmoded sensibility. In the *Lady Chatterley* incident there is no such nullifying doubt. Connie's tenderness is an instinctively recognized virtue, something morally axiomatic.

Lady Chatterley's Lover is a much better novel than *The Plumed Serpent* largely because of this return to immediate human sympathy. (Lawrence thought at one time of calling it "Tenderness.") It is also in general better written. Not since *Women in Love* had Lawrence taken so much care over one of his books. Three versions were written; the first has been printed as *The First Lady Chatterley* (1944); and the third is, of course, the one privately printed in Florence in 1928 and the subject of so much controversy.

Lawrence himself has made the most cogent defense of his book in the essays: "Pornography and Obscenity" and "A Propos of *Lady Chatterley's Lover*." Whatever remained to say has already been said by Edmund Wilson, Graham Hough, and Richard Hoggart.[6] There are two aspects of *Lady Chatterley* which have caused most debate: the frank descriptions of sexual intercourse and the use of the so-called four-letter words. The descriptions are an integral part of Lawrence's purpose. Far from being monotonously similar, as has been claimed, they represent different stages in the development of a physically passionate relationship. The four-letter words, which make only rare appearances in *The First Lady Chatterley* are less defensible. Lawrence's intention here is to rescue them from their odious associations and to restore them to decent usage. Language, however, is a socially created instrument; it is impossible for one individual to change its whole drift. These words are so degraded by common usage that they import meanings into Lawrence's novel that are completely alien to his passionately sincere treatment of his theme. Alternatively, they are reduced to the level of meaningless expletives, and as such are equally inappropriate for his purpose. What is remarkable is that he achieved so much in *Lady Chatterley's Lover* despite his misconceived crusade on behalf of the four-letter words.

In this novel Lawrence returns to his native region, and in the first version—though not, as already observed, in the final one—his presentation of working-class life is reminiscent of *Sons and Lovers*. Parkin, the original of Mellors, is a real member of the working class. He has not been lifted out of it by education and by life as an officer, nor does he wish to leave it. At the end of the novel he becomes a Communist because of a strong feeling of solidarity with his mates at the Sheffield steel works. One of the most interesting scenes—unfortunately, discarded in the final version—is that in which Connie visits the Tewson family with whom Parkin is staying in Sheffield. Bill Tewson, though earnest and naïve, is a genuine Yorkshireman (Lawrence has a sure sense for the difference between a Nottinghamshire and Derbyshire man and one from across the border). Tewson's shrewd, kindly wife and his children, the "high tea" with its quantities of tinned fruit and salmon, and the back street of terraced houses in which they live are all described with something of Dickensian warmth.

The final version loses this particular aspect of human sympathy, but in most other respects it is much superior to the first. Mrs. Bolton, the nurse who looks after Sir Clifford Chatterley, is the one character who still very obviously belongs to the earlier world. To many readers she is the most alive character in the book. She is a widow, and her marriage had been something real that leaves her with a reflected glow of life. But, as she grows more intimate with Sir Clifford, she shares with him a deterioration into perverted sexuality which is presented as an antithesis to the truly natural sexual relationship of Connie and Mellors.

The contrast between old, agricultural and new, industrial England becomes so sharp in the final version that there is no room for the aspect of working-class life represented by the Tewsons. Connie's drive from Wragby to Uthwaite is also given more prominence as a running commentary on the decay of the old England and evolves into a Wordsworthian lament for "what man has made of man." Mellors is now more evidently Lawrence's natural man, a survivor of real humanity in this industrial desert, who also offers some hope for the future. Connie, too, is a natural inhabitant of the older, pastoral world. She is described as "a ruddy, country-looking girl with soft brown hair and sturdy body, and slow movements, full of unusual energy. She had big, wondering eyes, and a soft mild voice, and seemed just to have come from her native village" (Chap. 1).

Sir Clifford represents the old English aristocracy. He seeks to preserve the woods and parkland of Wragby as part of his belief in "tradition," but this makes no common ground between

him and Connie. The very point of the discussion which they
have on this subject is to underline the sterility of Clifford's
attitude. And a later conversation between husband and wife
makes still clearer the contrast between them. Connie tells
Clifford, "You don't give one heart-beat of real sympathy.
And besides," she asks him, "who has taken away from the people
their natural life and manhood, and given them this industrial
horror?"

Clifford answers that the people have built Tevershall for
themselves, but his real reply is in his argument that the miners
are not men: "The masses were always the same, and will always
be the same. Nero's slaves were extremely little different from
our colliers or the Ford motor-car workmen. I mean Nero's mine
slaves and his field slaves. It is the masses: they are the un-
changeable" (Chap. 13). Clifford, who is immured in his hopelessly unimaginative class feeling, is scarcely aware that the
beings who live beyond his park gates belong to the same race
as himself. That Mellors can also give vent to detestation of the
whole human race unfortunately weakens the contrast between
his warmth and Clifford's inhumanity. But the character of
Connie is not spoilt by Lawrence's attributing such views to
her, and her warmth of feeling—the "tenderness"—which is
opposed to Clifford's coldness and insentience is realized in the
love between her and the gamekeeper.

IV Lady Chatterley's Lover: *Connie as a "Free" Woman*

Connie's love affair with Mellors is also in contrast to all the
previous experience she has had with men. It is a breakthrough
to something at last valid in the sexual relationship. The adolescent affairs of Connie and her sister Hilda with two German
boys had been based on "mental attraction." They "took the
sex-thrill as a sensation, and remained free," their real thrill
coming from the eternal talk.

The outbreak of war rushed them back to England where
they fell in with a liberal-minded Cambridge group "that stood
for 'freedom' and flannel trousers, and flannel shirts open at the
neck, and a well-bred sort of emotional anarchy." Among this
group Connie found Clifford. They married, and after one
month's honeymoon Clifford was paralyzed by a war wound.
The foundation of this relationship was once again mental—
"sex was merely an accident, or an adjunct, one of the curious

obsolete, organic processes which persisted in its own clumsiness, but was not really necessary"—and, consequently, Clifford's impotence made little or no difference.

On the vexed question of the paralysis Lawrence himself comments in "À Propos of *Lady Chatterley's Lover*" . . . "when I read the first version, I recognized that the lameness of Clifford was symbolic of the paralysis, the deeper emotional or passional paralysis, of most men of his sort or class today. I realized that it was perhaps taking an unfair advantage of Connie, to paralyse him technically. It made it so much more vulgar of her to leave him." [7]

Vulgarity, however, is of comparatively slight importance here. Connie is not lacking in pity for Clifford, but, like other Lawrentian heroines, she is caught up in a profounder issue involving life itself. What does call for criticism is Lawrence's handling, mainly in the latter part of the novel, of the condition that the paralysis symbolizes. Clifford is made to appear more and more bound within the hard shell of his ego-consciousness. Although this is consistent with his earlier character, it is savagely exaggerated. Moreover, Lawrence makes his own judgment too blatantly obvious.

Clifford took to writing stories of an intensely personal kind, confined to that "artificially-lighted stage" (the image is reminiscent of the pool of light in *The Rainbow*) which is modern existence. For Connie life became increasingly meaningless: " . . . it was all a dream; or rather it was like the simulacrum of reality. The oak-leaves were to her like oak-leaves seen ruffling in a mirror, she herself was a figure somebody had read about, picking primroses that were only shadows or memories, or words. No substance to her or anything . . . no touch, no contact! Only this life with Clifford, this endless spinning of webs of yarn, of the minutiae of consciousness . . ." (Chap. 2). Her condition began to approach the restlessness of Gudrun in *Women in Love*.

At this stage in her downward progress she met and had her affair with Michaelis. As a writer of bad plays, he recalls Loerke; and Lawrence describes him as having the same corrupt influence. On another level, his appeal—deliberately put over as a sexual trick—is that of the little boy lost; he exploits Connie's frustrated maternalism.

Michaelis is utterly selfish in his attitude to the sexual act, but there is something which implicates Connie as well. Each one regards the other as a mere provider of sensation. The nature of this relationship explains and justifies the satirically presented discussion in Chapter 4, where sex is reduced to the same level as talk: "We're free to talk to anybody; so why shouldn't we be free to make love to any woman who inclines us that way?" It has no deeper implications. Connie's increasing sense of unreality, culminating in the Michaelis affair, indicates the sterility to which such views lead; and, as typically advanced talk about sex, the discussion widens the significance of Connie's personal predicament so that it stands for that of a whole generation.

IV   Lady Chatterley's Lover: *Connie and Mellors*

While the Michaelis affair is still in being, but after sufficient space has been devoted to it to make its implications clear, Lawrence introduces Mellors. The actual entrance, as in a well written play, is carefully prepared. Clifford outlines his ideal of marriage as "the long, slow habit of intimacy" and suggests that Connie might perhaps have a child by some other, anonymous man without disturbing this relationship. Connie agrees, with the qualifications: "Only life may turn quite a new face on it all." At this moment a dog runs out from the wood where they are talking, and a man strides after: "It was only the new game-keeper, but he had frightened Connie, he seemed to emerge with such a swift menace. That was how she had seen him, like the sudden rush of a threat out of nowhere" (Chap. 5). This passage clearly enough heralds the complete change that Mellors brings about. He is a "threat" in the sense that he is to destroy her past and to give her a wholly new rhythm of life.

This rhythm is gradually built up. At her second encounter with Mellors, Connie sees something of his relationship to his child and his mother. He, too, has lost organic connections, and the effect is to make Connie feel that all the great words relating to love and family "were cancelled for her generation." And, when she next stumbles on him as he is washing himself, the shock that the sight of his white flesh gives her makes her pain-fully aware of her own body. Her deepest feelings and instinctive reactions thus begin to be connected with Mellors, and she finds herself more impatient with Clifford. Without knowing it, she develops an awareness of Mellors that makes it no longer pos-sible for her to keep her distance as Lady Chatterley, and this reaction leads on quite naturally to the scene at the hut with the chicks and to their first lovemaking.

It is Mellors' sympathy and instinctive realization of her plight that arouses his desire for her. His taking her is not felt as a sudden grasping at an opportunity for sexual relief, but as an act that realizes the latent bond between them. As Richard Hoggart says, there is an immense difference between this and the kind of sexual intercourse that is described in pornographic literature: "Here we feel a weight of respect—reverence, Lawrence would have said—for another; a sense of pity for another's grief and weakness; a recognition that our lives exist in time—have a past and future—rather than a shuttered focusing on to the thrill of the moment." [8]

Lawrence is honest, however. He does not pretend that their intercourse is in this instance physically satisfying to Connie. What gives her the peace she feels is the relaxation of her own will. And at their second lovemaking Connie is detached enough to find the man's movement ridiculous. This passage in Chapter 10 might be borne in mind by those who accuse Lawrence of humorless solemnity. She slightly resents, too, the way Mellors ignores her individual personality when making love to her, and she has a natural reaction towards the mental intimacy on which her marriage with Clifford has been based. Kate's relationship with Don Cipriano is echoed here, but the superiority of *Lady Chatterley* to *The Plumed Serpent* is evident. Mellors does not really ignore her as a person. He is nothing so banal as a "demon lover." The different, nonintimate quality which he manages to bring to their lovemaking has a convincing context; it grows out of warmth and compassion for the woman—if not the social being—that she is.

Connie's third experience with Mellors on her return from the visit to Mrs. Flint may seem to contradict this view of their relationship, since Mellors forces himself upon her. But Lawrence is, after all, tracing the development of a love affair in which a certain kind of man, as well as a certain kind of woman, is involved. Mellors has been extremely reluctant to let his desire be reawakened after what he has been through with his wife, Bertha; now that he is aroused, he finds his passion so strong as to be not altogether within his control. On this occasion the outcome of the lovemaking justifies him, but one of the things that he has to learn is how to live with a desire that is not at the time reciprocated: "Only at times, at times, the gap will be filled in. At times! But you have to wait for the times . . . . You can't force them." At the very end of the novel, when circumstances and Connie's pregnancy keep them temporarily apart, he has learned to accept his own statement.

The sexual relationship between Connie and Mellors reaches its maturity in Chapter 12. True to the incalculable rhythms of desire, Lawrence makes the tea which the lovers have together quite unsuccessful. Connie tells him about her intention to have a holiday in Venice, and Mellors is annoyed, thinking that he has been used as a means of begetting a child which the holiday will now cover up. Connie feels drawn to him again in the evening, but the earlier discord persists, and his lovemaking again seems ridiculous to her. Sex sinks in her mind to the level of a "function." Mellors realizes it is no good, and Lawrence's honesty and wish to present a relationship of real tenderness come together in one of the most moving passages of the novel:

'I . . . I can't love you,' she sobbed, suddenly feeling her heart breaking.

'Canna ter? Well, dunna fret! There's no law says as tha's got to. Ta'e it for what it is.'

He lay still with his hand on her breast. But she had drawn both her hands from him.

His words were small comfort. She sobbed aloud.

'Nay, nay!' he said. 'Ta'e the thick wi' th' thin. This wor' a bit o' thin for once.'

She wept bitterly, sobbing. 'But I want to love you, and I can't. It only seems horrid.'

He laughed a little, half bitter, half amused.

'It isna horrid,' he said, 'even if tha thinks it is. An' tha canna ma'e it horrid. Dunna fret thysen about lovin' me. Tha'lt niver force thysen to 't. There's sure to be a bad nut in a basketful. Tha mun ta'e th' rough wi' th' smooth.' (Chap. 12)

Connie's class image of Mellors imposes itself on her again; but, as he draws away, she suddenly clings to him and the positive rhythm of desire slowly begins to work in them. The emotion wells up from a deeper level than that on which their mutual irritation had existed. Lawrence's prose changes, too, with the new emotion from the staccato brevity of their mood of discord to the more sustained sentences and incantatory repetition which describe this renewal of love. The sea image which occurs in this passage is a recreation of the image of the River Trent used in *Sons and Lovers* to describe the lovemaking of Paul and Clara, but here it is more effectively controlled and more closely related to the preceding experience. Connie's experience has such depth that it brings her a sense of rebirth: "She was gone, she was not, and she was born: a woman." What is implicit in her sensitiveness to the chicks, and, of course, in the whole springtime setting of her affair with Mellors, is thus realized in herself; and at the end of the chapter her rebirth is again suggested through the kindling of an almost animistic feeling: "As she ran home in the twilight the world seemed a dream; the trees in the park seemed bulging and surging at anchor on a tide, and the heave of the slope to the house was alive" (Chap. 12). The "dream" now is no longer a "simulacrum of reality" as it was when her life was circumscribed by Clifford and his friends, but something "heaving" with life.

VI Lady Chatterley's Lover: *The Final Chapters*

After this scene the novel loses some of its freshness. The change from a dying world to a living one has been brought about. There are new experiences for Connie and Mellors to share, but they lack the significance of those they have been through. It may well have been Lawrence's intention to mark the maturity of their relationship by the "night of sensual passion" in Chapter 16 which, we are told, burns out "the deepest, oldest shames" in Connie and brings her "to the real bed-rock of her nature." This supposed purgation is, however, all too hectically proclaimed to compare with the real sense of renewal in the previous scene.

The scandal and the practical problems of arranging for divorce caused by the return of Bertha into Mellors' life provide more interesting material. These balance the idyllic period of "courtship" with a blunt recognition that conventional society cannot be wished away. But some of the incidents which belong to this part of the novel are in bad taste—for example, Mellors' rakish conversation with Connie's father in Chapter 18 and his attempt to connect an idealized version of the officer-man relationship with his love for Connie. And the letter with which the novel ends is for the most part a sorry mistake; it shifts much too far from genuine fiction towards naïve prescriptions for complex problems which Mellors does not begin to understand. It must be one of the most implausible love letters in English literature.

What most clearly indicates a lowering of imaginative intensity in the latter part of the novel is Lawrence's tendency to draw upon material already used in his earlier work. Connie's holiday in Venice is a repetition of the sort of satirical observation of the Englishman abroad done so well in *Aaron's Rod;* and Mrs. Bolton's success in making an efficient industrialist out of Clifford while reducing him to a childish emotional dependence on herself, though effective enough, is greatly inferior to Lawrence's treatment of that theme in *Women in Love.* Such passages suggest that the really original impetus had worked itself out; Lawrence was now merely going over what was for him old ground.

CHAPTER 7

The Tales

LAWRENCE'S tales are an important part of his total work. The
majority of them appeared in various collections throughout
his life: *The Prussian Officer*, 1914; *England, My England*, 1922;
The Ladybird (containing "The Ladybird," "The Fox," and "The
Captain's Doll," and taking its title in the American edition from
the latter tale), 1923; and *The Woman Who Rode Away*, 1928.
St. Mawr (with "The Princess") was published in 1925; *The Escaped Cock* (later titled *The Man Who Died*) in 1929; and *The
Virgin and the Gipsy* after Lawrence's death in 1930. A few other
stories appeared in posthumous volumes such as *Love Among
the Haystacks* (1930), *The Lovely Lady* (1933), and *A Modern
Lover* (1934). In many instances publication in magazines and
periodicals preceded hard-cover form so that the spread over
Lawrence's life is even more extensive than these dates suggest.

The stories themselves are of widely differing kinds. Some, like
"Strike-Pay" or "Two Blue Birds," are mere sketches; others—
most notably, "Daughters of the Vicar," "The Fox," "The Captain's Doll," "St. Mawr," and "The Virgin and the Gipsy"—are
short novels. Some are primarily realistic vignettes, and at the opposite extreme from these are tales which are virtually poems in
prose: "Sun," "The Woman Who Rode Away," and "The Escaped
Cock." Behind some of the tales is a genuinely original creative
impulse—and, where these tales are concerned, it is possible to
agree with those critics who find Lawrence aesthetically purer
and more satisfying in the stories than in the novels. But others
seem to be more potboilers or, at best, overspills from the experience that goes more completely into the novels. Lawrence seems
never to have considered the short story seriously as a form.
There are no new and striking critical pronouncements on it as
there are on the novel in his letters and articles, or on poetry in
his prefaces. It is true that he rarely engages in that direct lectur-

ing of his readers which can be so irritating in the novels; it is as if he realizes that the shorter form cannot afford such dilution. (Where a character such as Count Psanek in "The Ladybird" does become a spokesman for Lawrence's ideas, the intrusion is more objectionable than usual.) It is also true that some experimentation takes place in the tales, chiefly in the "poems in prose." But the virtues of most of the tales are those of the novels. The same kind of inspiration and the same manner of writing are evident in both.

I *The Early Tales*

The first volume, *The Prussian Officer*, contains stories which date from as early as 1907 when Lawrence entered a short-story competition in *The Nottingham Guardian*. One of these, "A Fragment of Stained Glass," was described by the adjudicator as "a tale of the escape of a serf remarkable for its vivid realism." [1] It is at least as remarkable for callow fantasy, suggesting the vein of immature romanticism that mars *The White Peacock* and some of the early poems. The realism is there, however, and "The White Stockings," another *Guardian* story to be printed in *The Prussian Officer*, shows Lawrence making much better use of his powers in this direction. This story concerns a flirtatious little schemer, Elsie; her slow husband; and an Edwardian ladykiller, Adams, who sends Elsie provocative Valentine presents. The best thing is the description of Elsie's dancing with Adams and voluptuously enjoying the spell which he casts over her. A faint hint is given here of Lawrence's more mature art.

"A Sick Collier," "Goose Fair," "Strike-Pay," "The Christening," "Odour of Chrysanthemums," and "Daughters of the Vicar" are all early tales of Lawrence's native Nottinghamshire and Derbyshire area; and they also have obvious connections with *Sons and Lovers*. They vary considerably among themselves, however. "The Christening" is an effective little sketch of a chapel-going, superior working-class family—the link with Mrs. Morel's aspirations is obvious—humbled by the misdemeanor of the younger daughter who gets herself pregnant by a local baker's assistant. The old father, who suffers from locomotor ataxia, but still has something of the patriarchal-prophetic air that his faith gives him, and the elder daughter, a schoolmistress with pretensions to refinement, are coolly but not unsympathetically presented.

"Odour of Chrysanthemums," first published in *The English*

Review in 1911, is perhaps Lawrence's earliest masterpiece. It was this story which attracted the attention of Ford Madox Ford. Apparently the opening paragraph was enough to convince Ford that he had found another genius. The memoir in which he tells this incident contains an excellent piece of practical criticism demonstrating the qualities which singled this work out for Ford from the run-of-the-mill stories he read every day. On the opening sentence he comments: ". . . at once you know that this fellow with the power of observation is going to write of whatever he writes about from the inside. . . . He sees the scene of his story exactly. He has an authoritative mind." [2] Ford notes, too, such vivid details as the colt outdistancing the engine "at a canter" and the gorse which "still flickered indistinctly in the raw afternoon."

What Ford does not mention—though it is very characteristic of the peculiarly Lawrentian sympathy which informs the passage—is the animation of the whole scene: the engine uttered "loud threats of speed," the trucks "thumped heavily," the dusk "crept into the spinney," the smoke "sank and cleaved to the rough grass," the pit-bank had "flames like red sores licking its ashy sides," and the winding engine of the colliery "rapped out its little spasms." The scene has a distinct personality, and this not only makes it an exceptionally vivid piece of descriptive writing, but also provides an implicit contrast with the lives of the main characters of the story. Elizabeth Bates is married to a miner who habitually goes straight from the pit to the public house. He isolates himself from his family, and his wife responds with bitterness and resentment. The vitality of the background against which they live out their lives thus throws into relief the almost bankrupt condition of their marriage.

An anonymous woman walking along the railway line in the first paragraph of the story is described as stepping aside to let the engine pass, and so being "insignificantly trapped between the jolting black waggons and the hedge." This, too, has its imaginative link with the rest of the tale. It suggests the trap of meaningless routine into which Elizabeth's life has sunk and is a muted anticipation of the way in which her miner-husband meets his death—trapped by a fall of coal which catches him between itself and the coal face. This poetically suggestive theme reaches its climax when Elizabeth wonders to herself over the dead body of her husband. She realizes that they "had denied each other life."

Lawrence thus takes the reader to one of his central insights about the relation between man and woman, but he skillfully makes it an organic part of the region in which the pair have lived out their lives.

"Daughters of the Vicar" is a more ambitious tale. The choice of husbands made by the two Lindley daughters involves two different and unremittingly opposed conceptions of marriage. Mary (she owes something to Dorothea in George Eliot's *Middlemarch*) is a highminded girl who allows principle to prevail over instinct. She feels a physical repugnance for the Reverend Mr. Massy, but she decides to marry him because she respects his sense of duty. Her sister, Louisa, however, abides by instinct. She declares that she would have nothing whatever to do with Mr. Massy, and her own choice is in favor of the socially inferior but vital Alfred. Money comes into this contrast as well, for, in choosing Mr. Massy, Mary is also patching up the decayed fortunes of her family.

Lawrence presents the choices of the two daughters as moral issues, involving allegiance on the one hand to "abstract goodness" and on the other to the "blood." What the blood knows to be right is shown to be the proper criterion. The strength of the story, however, is not in this implicit thesis, but in the faithfulness with which the feelings of the two girls are rendered. Their conflicting notions of "goodness" are dramatically realized, especially in the scenes where they discuss the implications of Mr. Massy's visit to Alfred's dying father.

Mr. Massy is not created with the same sympathetic insight. He is a piece of machinery rather than a character; and, by the end of the tale, his ridiculous obsession with the baby's health reduces him to the level of caricature. Yet he is an embodiment of Mary's ideal of the good, and this fact has a boomerang effect on the way Mary herself is presented. Somewhat unfairly, she is made to share the opprobrium that Lawrence's one-sided presentation brings on Mr. Massy.

Nevertheless, Mary is still seen with the novelist's eye. Lawrence sees a certain "heroism" in her, even though his own siding with Louisa is apparent. The limitations that Mary's family and class impose upon her are taken into consideration, and "the millstone of poverty," which accounts for Mrs. Lindley's willingness to see her daughter married to Mr. Massy although she, too, finds him repugnant, is far from being sentimentally ignored. One of the virtues of this tale is that it reckons with the reality of such problems and conveys with distaste, but also with a sympathetic inwardness, the peculiar snobbishness of lower-middle-class English provincial life at the beginning of the twentieth century.

The different "heroism" of Louisa is that she has the courage to break through this barrier of snobbishness and to find her real mate in Alfred Durant. Lawrence approves of her special combination of practicality and romanticism. She and Mary are an interesting variation on Jane Austen's sense and sensibility, and the tale ends with a piece of comedy, effectively dramatized through dialogue, which suggests that Lawrence—despite his rude words about her—did not fail to learn a great deal from Jane Austen.

Two quite different stories—although they appear in the same volume as "Odour of Chrysanthemums" and "Daughters of the Vicar"—are "The Prussian Officer" and "The Thorn in the Flesh." These belong to the period of Lawrence's first visit to Germany in 1912, and they reflect the sadistic militarism of the Prussians. "The Thorn in the Flesh" tells how a young soldier panics when climbing a scaling ladder, but has his self-respect restored by the love of his sweetheart. Its chief merit is its descriptions of intense physical sensation, in which respect it is similar to "The Prussian Officer." In this more important tale, the homosexual interest felt by the officer for his orderly conflicts with the social and disciplinary distance put between them by the rigid military caste system, and this barrier generates an intolerable tension which Lawrence communicates with almost painful immediacy. The officer and man are of contrasting temperaments: one is "a man of passionate temper, who had always kept himself suppressed"; the other "seemed to live out his warm, full nature." This contrast gives a very necessary psychological coherence to the officer's bullying of the man and to the man's final resort to brutal murder, and it also makes the last sentence an unusually telling one: "The bodies of the two men lay together, side by side, in the mortuary, the one white and slender, but laid rigidly at rest, the other looking as if every moment it must rouse into life again, so young and unused, from a slumber."

II *The "Compulsion" Theme*

In "The Prussian Officer" Lawrence displays a violent perversion of natural vitality. The officer mistreats his orderly in spite of himself—it is not that he lacks self-control, in the usual sense, but that he is carried along helplessly by the stream into which his life has set. The profoundest outrage that he commits is against himself. Lawrence is becoming aware now—one sees it even more clearly, of course, in the novels of this period—of certain laws of life which may run quite contrary to established social patterns and to the conscious desires of individuals, but which cannot be thwarted without bringing disaster.

This theme of "compulsion" is the subject of a group of tales: "You Touched Me," "Samson and Delilah," "The Horse Dealer's Daughter," "Fanny and Annie" (all from the *England, My England* volume), and "The Fox" (from *The Ladybird*). In "You Touched Me," Matilda, the daughter of a pottery manufacturer whose business has closed down, is forced into marriage with a charity-institution boy who has been adopted by her father. She and her sister are both threatened with exclusion from their father's will if she refuses to marry him. It is as if Lawrence has deliberately chosen a plot which will excite the ordinary reader's disgust in order to show the ruthless disregard of life for gentler, humanitarian considerations. Hadrian, the charity boy, feels that he has a right to Matilda because she touched him one night and woke him from his sleep, even though Matilda explains that she accidentally mistook him for her father: "If you wake a man up, he can't go to sleep again because he's told to." "Touch," for Lawrence, is a form of physical contact that transcends sensuous experience and evokes powers that lie beneath everyday consciousness. It is essential to the success of the story "You Touched Me" that this should be communicated to the readers. Matilda's accidental touching of Hadrian is meant to be as profoundly non-accidental as a Freudian slip. But Lawrence does not altogether succeed here. He shows Matilda already betraying an awareness of Hadrian before the touch and the proposal occur, and his description of the touch ("Delicately, her fingers met the nose and the eyebrows. . . . A sort of surprise stirred her, in her entranced state.") hints at the deeper force at work; but not enough is done to counterbalance the impression of brute will—even more on the part of the father than of Hadrian—by which Matilda's acceptance is brought about.

"The Horse Dealer's Daughter" avoids this distastefulness. When Dr. Fergusson saves Mabel from drowning herself, and she asks, "Do you love me, then?" the superficial appearance which the compulsion takes on is that of emotional bullying entangled with the doctor's professional concern. But his previous awareness of Mabel has been adequately stressed, and the whole episode of the rescue is given far more narrative prominence. Lawrence reckons with the struggle that goes on in the doctor—his initial bewilderment and his revulsion from the woman's emotional demand give way to the stronger force of unrecognized attraction—which makes his surrender at once more convincing and more humane.

The compulsion exercised in "Samson and Delilah" and in "Fanny and Annie" is saved from seeming harsh by the comic element in these two stories. In "Samson and Delilah" a husband forces himself on his wife, the landlady of a public house, after a sixteen-year absence. He is tied up and thrown out by some soldiers, only to find that his wife has left the back door open so that he can creep in again. In "Fanny and Annie" Fanny has to give up her hopes of a more refined life and marry an old flame who has, during her absence, made another woman (Annie) pregnant. In a splendid scene the lover is denounced by Annie's mother before a chapel congregation. This "comedown" makes Fanny great sport for the local gossips, but she sticks to her lover all the same.

"The Fox" immediately reveals its superiority to all the tales which precede it by the assured quality of its style. The early paragraph describing March, who along with Banford is making a not very successful attempt to run Bailey Farm, is an example of this assured style. March plays the man in this ménage of two girls, but she is not really a masculine type, and her consequent ambiguity is beautifully caught by Lawrence. Her movements are "easy and confident," but she is clearly not in her element. The halfhearted attempt which she and Banford make at farming —wittily, but not unsympathetically, described—is also connected with this suggestion of something odd and unnatural. Their whole enterprise, a deliberate assertion of female independence, is subtly undermined by the natural laws which they try to ignore.

Their chief enemy is the fox. March sees it one day, but is not quick enough to shoot it because of a momentary paralysis of her will:

She lowered her eyes, and suddenly saw the fox. He was looking up at her. His chin was pressed down, and his eyes were looking up. They met her eyes. And he knew her. She was spellbound—she knew he knew her. So he looked into her eyes, and her soul failed her. He knew her, he was not daunted.

She struggled, confusedly she came to herself, and saw him making off, with slow leaps over some fallen boughs, slow, impudent jumps. Then he glanced over his shoulder, and ran smoothly away. She saw his brush held smooth like a feather, she saw his white buttocks twinkle. And he was gone, softly, soft as the wind.

The impression made by the fox is lasting. Its image comes into March's mind at unexpected moments, especially when she is daydreaming—"then it was the fox which somehow dominated her unconsciousness."

All this is a prelude to the arrival of Henry, the destroyer of the relationship between March and Banford. Like Hadrian in "You Touched Me," he is an intruder (though, ironically, more unwelcome at first to March than to Banford), but his appearance has been well prepared for. To March, he incarnates the fox, which gives him a peculiar power over her. When he stays the night, she dreams of the fox and of wanting to touch it, but of being bitten and seared by its brush. And she cannot shake off Henry's influence. On realizing the threat that he constitutes to their way of life, Banford tries to alienate March from him; and, though she seems to be succeeding, Henry's unconscious hold over March cannot be broken. In the end Banford is killed by a falling tree, seemingly as a result of her own willfulness, but really because of Henry's rooted enmity towards her. He is, again, an embodiment of what in these "compulsion" tales is seen as the necessary ruthlessness of life.

The fineness of "The Fox," however, is not only in its symbolic treatment of "compulsion" but in the texture of its realism as well. Lawrence may make ludicrous blunders over such details as how a soldier approaches an officer and applies for special leave, but he accurately reproduces the daily routine of March and Banford (Lawrence, of course, had firsthand experience of farm life, and little knowledge of life in the army), the way they speak to one another, and the way Henry speaks to, and thinks of, them. As a combination of symbolism and realism, it is the best of Lawrence's tales. The realism makes the fox and all it stands for seem an essential part of, rather than an abstraction from, life; and the symbolism adds to the faithful reflection of ordinary existence a dimension which deepens the very notion of the "real."

III *"The Ladybird" and "The Captain's Doll"*

"The Ladybird" and "The Captain's Doll," the two tales, or short novels, published along with "The Fox" in the volume of 1923, are linked with it by their preoccupation with male domination and female submission. The first is a rather tedious failure; the second, a considerable success, is unique among Lawrence's fiction as a work of pure comedy.

"The Ladybird" is not so much a tale as a fictionalized essay about the mystic glamor of a little Bavarian prisoner of war and the spell which he casts over a rather spoiled English beauty, Lady Daphne. She becomes bored with the "adoration-lust" of her husband, Basil, who in spite of himself induces a psychic illness in her. Count Psanek, the prisoner, brings her relief from her nervous tension and a new, strange feeling of *insouciance*. She falls in love with him, but he does not run off with her. Instead he counsels her to stay with her husband as a daytime wife, but to remain "the night-wife of the ladybird"—the ladybird being the ancient symbol of the Psanek family. Lawrence tries to present both the husband and the Count as "decent" (in the very English sense of that word) gentlemen, and this gets him into an unhappy tangle such as does not happen when his romantic outsider is a gypsy or a gamekeeper and when the Establishment figure is a vicarage family or a Sir Clifford. Even more disturbing is the insincere, fabricated serenity and semitragic wisdom that is suggested by the peculiar style in which "The Ladybird" is written. Count Psanek is so obviously a thin disguise for Lawrence himself, and his male supremacy is so much talked about and so little realized that one is tempted to regard the whole tale as a piece of wish fulfillment, the spuriousness of which is revealed in the pseudopoetic prose.

"The Captain's Doll" is a very welcome contrast to "The Ladybird." The character of Hannele clearly owes a great deal to Frieda. There is nothing maudlin about her as there is about Lady Daphne, and, when she becomes involved in a tussle with her Scottish captain over the problem of the "maistrie," her reactions are far more convincingly feminine.

One of the most attractive features of this tale is that neither Hannele nor Captain Hepburn is put in the right. Lawrence takes a refreshingly comic view of them both. From the first, when Hannele is seen putting the finishing touches to the little doll

replica of Hepburn, her rather complacently detached appreciation of her lover is humorously suggested. Her sister's admiring
comment—"Exactly him. Just as finished as he is. Just as complete. He is just like that: finished off"—has the right double-
edged touch. But it hits at something in Hepburn as well as Hannele. They are both of them a little unreally self-contained. It is
the sister again who follows up this point with a comment on the
captain's room: "Beautiful! But Beautiful! Such good taste! A
man, and such good taste! No, they don't need a woman. No, look
here, Martin, the Captain Hepburn has arranged all this room
himself. Here you have the man. Do you see? So simple, yet so
elegant. He needs no woman."

Hannele is both fascinated and annoyed by Hepburn: "she
loved the spell that bound her. But also she didn't love it." Hepburn himself, since he can exert this spell over Hannele, has to be
taken seriously; but, when his wife—who has heard rumors of an
affair—turns up to put him in order, he cuts a ridiculous figure.
He is deflated to the level of a perfectly ordinary, "nice" English
husband.

The tea party at which Mrs. Hepburn "tackles" Hannele is one
of Lawrence's best bits of comedy. Lawrence handles very skillfully the moment when Mrs. Hepburn seems about to tell Hannele that she knows very well who her husband's mistress is, only
to veer off into the hilarious mistake of thinking the mistress is
not Hannele but her sister. Her practical astuteness is, after all,
very limited. And this has its effect, too, on Hannele's—and the
reader's—opinion of Hepburn. She cannot avoid thinking of him
now as "The husband of the little lady!"

Lawrence conveniently gets rid of Mrs. Hepburn by a Fors-
terian death—she falls out of her hotel bedroom window. The
consequence is unexpected, however, "Jack hath not Jill." Instead of taking advantage of their freedom, the lovers part, until
Hepburn comes round to thinking that he might like to marry
Hannele—on terms of her submission to him as an impersonal
male—and traces her whereabouts by means of the doll. The
latter section in which Hepburn woos Hannele afresh, but with
an obstinate refusal to accept any of the normal conventions of
wooing, is lacking in the concentration and wit of the first. Their
long climb together up to the glacier dilutes the comedy too
much, although it is punctuated with quarrels that recapture
some of the earlier humor.

Nothing conclusive emerges from their incongruous debate on love and marriage. Hepburn rather loses his original character, merging into Lawrence himself; and he uses arguments that read like a parody of those used by Birkin–Lawrence in *Women in Love* (to which Hannele retorts with the vigor of Ursula-Frieda). In the end, Hepburn wins a very doubtful promise from Hannele. He insists that she must not only love but obey him, as in the marriage service. Her answer is: "I won't say it *before* the marriage service. I needn't, need I?" One is left with the quiet impression that Hepburn will have to be content with the very real woman she is rather than with the conjectural female he would like her to be—which is a proper conclusion for a comedy.

IV Satire and "England, My England"

In the tales Lawrence is generally more inclined to satire than to comedy—or   at least, to a sardonic form of humor which is rather different from the sense of the ridiculous and the ironic which permeates "The Captain's Doll." One sees this satiric strain developing as early as "England, My England," which first appeared in *The English Review* of October, 1915. The Egbert of this story is a charming but ineffectual young man who lets himself be financially dependent on his father-in-law. The man who does not support his wife and family out of his own income invariably earns Lawrence's contempt.

In some way Egbert is also connected with primitive England. The old Hampshire cottage where he spends most of his time is situated among "shaggy gorse commons, and marshy, snake-infested places near the foot of the south downs. The spirit of place lingering on primeval, as when the Saxons came, so long ago." Egbert and his family, however, represent the old England in decay, and it is the accompanying loss of self-respect and vigor that the satire reveals, often through trivial, but suggestive details. The children, for example are spoiled: "There was a sound of children's voices calling and talking: high, childish, girlish voices, slightly didactic and tinged with domineering: 'If you don't come quick, nurse, I shall run out there to where there are snakes.' And nobody had the sangfroid to reply: 'Run then, little fool.' It was always, 'No, darling. Very well, darling. In a moment, darling. Darling, you *must* be patient.'" And, again, Egbert's interests are those of the dilettante. His gardening is successful in producing flowers, but his more solid efforts are nothing more than "little temporary contrivances."

The first serious consequence of Egbert's weakness is the laming of his little girl when she falls on a sickle which Egbert has left in the garden. The disintegration of the family follows, and at last Egbert, having joined the army, goes to Flanders, where he is killed by a German shell. Not altogether convincingly, Lawrence seems to imply that Egbert brings his death on himself. Rather vaguely the whole war, it is suggested, is the death of the old England, of which Egbert's story is symptomatic.

The impression left by "England, My England" is of something brittle, unformed, and rather jeering in tone. These are faults which mar several of the satirical stories—"The Border Line," "Jimmy and the Desperate Woman," "The Last Laugh," "The Princess" (all 1924), "Smile" (ca. 1925-6), and "Two Blue Birds" (1926). A sadistic element is noticeable, too; it is different from the harshness present in the "compulsion" tales, which is the harshness of nature, and from the sadism of "The Prussian Officer," which is diagnostically presented. "The Border Line" is the most distasteful of these tales. The concluding episode in which the ghost of Katherine's first husband prevents her from saving the life of her second excites positive revulsion. The intention, clearly enough, is that Alan, the first husband, has returned to give her new life; but the effect is to make her seem bereft of normal pity and humanity.

In "The Princess" one encounters a more complex mixture of experience. A spoiled rich girl, Dollie, makes a trip to some remote mountains in New Mexico, where her guide, Romero, rapes her. The jeering kind of satire is evident in the presentation of Dollie as the "flower of maidenhood," but by insisting on the continuance of the mountain trip, even without her companion, Miss Cummins, Dollie displays a selfishness and obstinacy that make the disastrous outcome largely her own fault. The "compulsion" theme is also present. In violating her, Romero nevertheless gets hold of "some unrealised part of her which she never wished to realise." And, finally, the New Mexico setting and the Indian blood in Romero's veins introduce that genuine feeling for primitive landscapes and primitive man which was the essence of the American experience for Lawrence.

V   *"St. Mawr"*

Two important tales emerge from the combination of the satirical mode and the American experience: "St. Mawr" and "The
Woman Who Rode Away." Yet they are very different from one
another. In "St Mawr" the satirical mode is more prominent; in
"The Woman Who Rode Away" it is the American experience
that outweighs, and almost extinguishes, the satire. In both tales
Lawrence is manifestly trying to deepen the satire to the level of
a radical criticism of life, the nature of which is indicated by
F. R. Leavis' linking of "St Mawr" with *The Waste Land;* but
Lawrence is not altogether successful. In "St. Mawr" a vein of
misanthropy causes him to load the dice against certain of his
characters, and in "The Woman Who Rode Away" the very bril-
liance of the poetic style, which enables him to recreate the
American experience, carries him beyond the range of the critical
intelligence.

"St. Mawr" is a peculiarly difficult work to criticize honestly
because of the constantly conflicting reactions of admiration and
disgust which it excites. Its power is undeniable. The sharpness
of the satirical insight into the whole world of Rico, the Manbys,
and Dean Vyner compels attention to their essential sterility.
(The fact that Lawrence betrays some ignorance of what "horsey"
society is really like does not greatly matter.) But the sharpness
of Lawrence's criticism is impaired by being put into the mouths
of Rico's wife, Lou, and her mother, Mrs. Witt. These two
women are among Lawrence's most unpleasant characters. Considered simply as a created character, Mrs. Witt, who has a more
powerful personality than her daughter, is a tremendous achievement. It is not any failure in realizing her that is disturbing, but
the fact that we are asked to associate her in some way with
sanity and life amid a world of hypocrisy and evil. Moreover, her
own and Lou's experience—though real enough for the sort of
persons they are—does not have the representative quality that
appears to be claimed for it. England cannot be presumed sterile
on the basis of what they have seen, for they have seen comparatively little.

Lawrence does not hide what is objectionable about Mrs. Witt.
Her life is as revoltingly geared to sheer will as Hermione's in
Women in Love. She professes to love "real men"; but, "on close
contact, it was difficult to define what she meant by 'real' men.

She never met any." Her actual interest in other people is to force them to bow to her cold, domineering will. She embodies the vulgar confidence of the hard-bitten, much traveled, wealthy American matron; and, though professing to despise the society creatures around her, she evidently derives great satisfaction from being able to insult and snub them.

It is difficult to believe in Mrs. Witt's living at the New Mexico ranch, to which she and Lou retire at the end of the tale, away from the socialites who feed her contempt; and Lawrence wisely does not pretend that she shares Lou's enthusiasm for the new life. Yet the way has to some extent been prepared by the collapse of will in Mrs. Witt. In the groom, Lewis, she at last does find a "man" (such is the intention, though Lewis is a poor realization of this ideal), only to have her offer of marriage rejected by him. The *cul de sac* into which her will drives her is thus made clear to her, and she abandons all decisionmaking.

The most compelling section of "St. Mawr" is that which describes the New Mexico ranch (it was Lawrence's own) and the successive attempts made by a schoolmaster and a trader who has a New England wife to impose some kind of rudimentary civilization on raw, unsympathetic nature. This process involves both creation and destruction:

> For all savagery is half-sordid. And man is only himself when he is fighting on and on, to overcome the sordidness.
>
> And every civilisation, when it loses its inward vision and its cleaner energy, falls into a new sort of sordidness, more vast and more stupendous than the old savage sort. An Augean stables of metallic filth.
>
> And all the time, man has to rouse himself afresh, to cleanse the new accumulations of refuse. To win from the crude wild nature the victory and the power to make another start, and to cleanse behind him the century-deep deposits of layer upon layer of refuse: even of tin cans.

Mrs. Witt's malevolence and destructiveness are apparently meant to be seen as part of this process. Her positive contribution is the effort she makes to save the stallion, St. Mawr—symbol of pure, animal vitality—first from being shot, and then from being gelded. Dean and Mrs. Vyner, who want to destroy the horse, are crushed by Mrs. Witt; the tea party at which she demonstrates her deadly social skill is far more devastating than the one in "The Captain's Doll," and also more satirically biased. It is a scene giving ample evidence of Lawrence's great dramatic skill—

it is almost theatrical—yet rather obviously one-sided. Dean Vyner has a good case which Lawrence gives no chance. Mrs. Witt's version of how St. Mawr kicked a young man and threw Rico (that Rico was to blame, not the horse) becomes the tale's version; and, although this strengthens Mrs. Witt's claim to be seen as creatively destructive, it exposes Lawrence himself to the charge of evading the nastiness inherent in this version by denying the more normally human view an adequate spokesman.

It is impossible, however, to accept all the corrosive outbursts of Mrs. Witt as creatively destructive; and, what is more damaging to the central theme of the tale, it is impossible to accept her and Lou's attitude towards St. Mawr. Lou dislikes men altogether and tells her mother: "After all, St. Mawr is better. And I'm glad if he gives them a kick in the face." This is not merely a phrase, but a comment on what has happened, and it is confirmed by her indifference to the young man who is kicked and to her own husband who is more seriously hurt—an indifference which seems to carry Lawrence's approval. (The concern shown by other characters is presented as effete and radically insincere. No one is allowed normal, decent feelings.) The whole story is so cast that it even appears that Lou's giving St. Mawr to Rico—in full knowledge of the horse's vicious streak (it has already killed two men) and with an implied subconscious urge to destroy her husband—also carries Lawrence's approval. Lewis tells her that St. Mawr is all right if met halfway, "But," is the comment, "half-way across from our human world to that terrific equine twilight was not a small step. It was a step, she knew, that Rico could never take. She knew it. But she was prepared to sacrifice Rico."

It is a tribute to Lawrence's power as an artist that he can give plausibility to the improbable story of a wife's sacrificing her husband for the sake of a horse and enlisting her mother's aid to transport the horse to a remote ranch in the Southwest. Lawrence overcomes this improbability by the forcefulness of his presentation of St. Mawr. Its color, its coat, its gallop, its neigh, its shying, its rearing—all are concretely there. As in the *Birds, Beasts and Flowers* poems, Lawrence reveals his uncanny ability to communicate the unique, independent reality of an animal. But the amount of space devoted to the horse itself is not great. It is the focus for what interests Lawrence rather than the actual subject. By fulfilling its nature as a horse, St. Mawr provides a standard of judgment for man's failure to fulfill his nature as a man. "It seems to me," says Lou:

there's something else besides mind and cleverness, or niceness or cleanness. Perhaps it is the animal. Just think of St. Mawr! I've thought so much about him. We call him an animal, but we never know what it means. He seems a far greater mystery to me than a clever man. He's a horse. Why can't one say in the same way, of a man: *He's a man?* There seems no mystery in being a man. But there's a terrible mystery in St. Mawr.

Lou's problem is the same as that of Ursula in *The Rainbow*, and the outraged horses at the end of *The Rainbow* are precursors of St. Mawr. The importance of St. Mawr lies in what it makes Lou perceive, and the imaginative justification that it gives to her otherwise incredible behavior. The attitudes of the characters towards St. Mawr become a means of defining their instinctive acceptance or rejection of evil. This comes clearly to the surface when, immediately after Rico's accident, Lou has "a vision of evil." The Manby girls, particularly Flora, frivolous and harmless though they may seem, share this evil because they can see in St. Mawr nothing but a beast for their use, which may be gelded if that will make it more useful.

Nevertheless, Lawrence himself virtually drops the horse when he gets his two main characters to America. The proper study of mankind remains man. This had been made clear by Lou before: "I don't want to be an animal like a horse or a cat or a lioness. . . ." And in America the emphasis of the tale significantly shifts not only from St. Mawr but from Lou and Mrs. Witt also to the previous owners of their New Mexico ranch—an unnamed schoolteacher and a New England housewife. Both of these are infinitely more attractive, if only sketches and not fully developed characters, than either Lou or Mrs. Witt. The New England housewife gives Lawrence a pretext for taking a sideswipe at American transcendentalism, but that is much less interesting and important than the bristlingly alive description of the New Englander's struggle to tame some part of a terribly nonhuman and untameable landscape. Nature ferociously comes into its own; and the human beings who engage in this struggle command a respect that none of the major characters can begin to approach.

The struggle must constantly be renewed. This concept, too,

Lawrence conveys with the same astonishing immediacy. That Lou's arrival should be presented as "new blood to the attack" is, however, an attempt to credit her with a capacity for tough, hard living which she does not possess. And her problem is not of the same kind as that faced by the frontiersman. If the one is a metaphor for the other, Lawrence still fails to make the connection convincing. It is Mrs. Witt's comment, very much in her old, characteristic vein, that sticks in the reader's mind: " 'Well, Louise,' she said. 'I am glad you feel competent to cope with so much hopelessness and so many rats.' "

VI *"The Woman Who Rode Away"*

"The Woman Who Rode Away" is only a quarter the length of "St. Mawr." Clearly a tale and not a short novel, it is limited to the telling of one episode. It runs to as much as thirty-two pages, not because of the amount of material to be conveyed, or the complexity to be unfolded (in this tale Lawrence deliberately rejects the modern preference for "complexity"), but because of the space required to build up the trancelike condition of "barbaric ecstasy" which is its peculiar achievement.

The method employed by Lawrence is to combine repetition with alliterative and assonantal association of words so that, instead of striking separately and independently on the consciously discriminating mind, they fuse into a poetic matrix. This method is, of course, the basic one in all Lawrence's prose and verse, and "The Woman Who Rode Away" could be regarded simply as one of the most striking examples of his general style. But there is also some justification for regarding it as a tale in which the style is more than usually intrinsic to the special kind of task that is being performed. The nature of that task is indicated in the title: the description of a journey from a familiar place to one that is remote and overwhelmingly "other," and involving a complete reversal of what is normally taken for reality. This process of transformation cannot be explained; it must be recreated through the evocative power of words. This being so, the kind of analysis appropriate to "The Woman Who Rode Away" is different from that used for the rest of the tales. Language, rather than character and incident, is the natural focus of attention, and power of suggestion is more important than the verisimilitude usually demanded of prose fiction.

The story begins in a casual, off-hand manner:

She had thought that this marriage, of all marriages, would be an adventure. Not that the man himself was exactly magical to her. A little, wiry, twisted fellow, twenty years older than herself, with brown eyes and greying hair, who had come to America a scrap of a wastrel, from Holland, years ago, as a tiny boy, and from the gold-mines of the west had been kicked south into Mexico, and now was more or less rich, owning silver-mines in the wilds of the Sierra Madre: it was obvious that the adventure lay in his circumstances, rather than his person. But he was still a little dynamo of energy, in spite of accidents survived, and what he had accomplished he had accomplished alone. One of those human oddments there is no accounting for.

The loose syntax; the tendency to imitate the scrappiness of conversation, together with its slightly exaggerated slanginess ("kicked south into Mexico"); the tinge of mockery—all tie this opening paragraph to the familiar, everyday world. The phrase, "little dynamo of energy"—almost, but not quite, a dead metaphor—connects with the mechanistic, engineering world that is introduced in the next few paragraphs. "Adventure" and "magical" are negatived, as much by their general context as by the negative formulae in which they are placed; but they also slip into the stream of the tale to find their significance later.

The style remains the same while the tale is set in the area of the disused silver-works, though short brittle sentences are interspersed, adding a crackle of nervous tension. It is the realization of a certain kind of death (symbolized by the dead dog lying in the marketplace), which is echoed when the woman, on her way to find the Chilchuis, hears "a great crash at the centre of herself, which was the crash of her own death."

As the woman (she is always referred to impersonally) sets out on her journey, the language becomes more fluent. There is no obvious change, however. Short sentences are still frequent, but adjectival qualification increases, and the syntax acquires the looseness of relaxation rather than of broken conversation. The woman slips into an acquiescent, almost fatalistic mood.

Her meeting with the three Indians involves dialogue which is seemingly naturalistic, but creates the strange effect of leaving far more unsaid than is said. Just as the woman's anger when her horse is beaten forward proves to be futile against the impersonal intentness of the Indians, so spoken words seem to be far less than unspoken implications. On reaching the village, the woman is met by an old chief who questions her about her purpose in coming there. Her answers are again laconic, but now with a distinct ambiguity, of which she herself is half aware and half ignorant, as if powerless to control the meaning that flows through them. Later she is asked, ". . . do you bring your heart to the god of the Chilchui?" and her "Tell him yes" is spoken "automatically," putting the seal to the dangerous ambiguity in her answers. Morally this sort of thing is a little disturbing. There is an evasiveness about it, almost as if Lawrence were cruelly betraying the woman. Yet it cannot be said that Lawrence does not know what he is doing. He actually describes the Indians as being evasive to the woman, and she somehow falls in with the mood. The creating of this state of affairs is a *tour de force*, involving a deliberate suppression of the conscious critical faculty of which one cannot approve, but this does not alter the fact that the artistic method is accomplished and highly effective. A half-unwilling suspension of disbelief is forced on the reader.

The Indians imprison the woman and give her a drugged drink which induces a trancelike condition. In a sense, however, she is already in a trance, so that the drink only intensifies her mood. Under its influence she experiences what is almost a mystical revelation:

Afterwards she felt a great soothing languor steal over her, her limbs felt strong and loose and full of languor, and she lay on her couch listening to the sounds of the village, watching the yellowing sky, smelling the scent of burning cedar-wood, or pine-wood. So distinctly she heard the yapping of tiny dogs, the shuffle of far-off feet, the murmur of voices, so keenly she detected the smell of smoke, and flowers, and evening falling, so vividly she saw the one bright star infinitely remote, stirring above the sunset, that she felt as if all her senses were diffused on the air, that she could distinguish the sound of evening flowers unfolding, and the actual crystal sound of the heavens, as the vast belts of the world-atmosphere slid past one another, and as if the moisture ascending and the moisture descending in the air resounded like some harp in the cosmos.

These two slow, undulating sentences—somewhat reminiscent of Tennyson's *The Lotos Eaters*, but less obvious in technique—are intentionally remote from the prose of the beginning of the tale. They are not, however, stylistically the absolute antithesis of the opening. To be that, they would have to be syntactically very different—complex, involuted, magisterially controlled—

whereas these are still syntactically loose. The movement of the first sentence is an overlapping one, aided by repetition. "Afterwards she felt" is paralleled in "her limbs felt;" "languor" is simple repetition, with "full" aurally related to "felt" and "loose" to "soothing"; the second half of the sentence makes use of comparison to give a triple wave effect—"listening . . . ," "watching . . . ," "smelling. . . ." Several other present participles prolong the impetus of this movement into the next sentence, which is thus integrated with its predecessor, even though its own structure is rather different. The thrice-repeated "So" pattern is technically speaking periodic and is followed by a long serpentine coiling of result clauses. It belongs, however, to the kind of periodicity found in Spenser's *Epithalamion* rather than in Milton or in Dr. Johnson. The units into which it falls are in themselves fairly brief and not intellectually taxing. The syntactical design provides them with a purpose which makes them flow forward effortlessly, and the alliterative "f's" and "s's," besides creating the muted sound of the harp image at the end of the sentence, also contribute to this flow.

Although this passage describes the effect of the strange drink which the woman is given, the style does not isolate it from the rest of the narrative. The more fluent syntax, the repetitions, and the aural music affect the whole of the latter section of the tale. Certain words such as "soft," "smile" or "smiling," "exultance," and "dark" (frequently contrasted with "white" or "snow") constantly recur as a leitmotiv. Others simply recur a number of times at one particular point. "Languor," for instance, flows over from the above passage on to the next page or two, and the word "fox," four times repeated, adds a peculiar intensity to the description of the Indians' dancing. The repetitions rise to an hypnotic pitch when the woman is bathed and anointed for the sacrifice, and their impetus is not lost as the procession moves towards the cave of ice. The sentences become shorter again because of the dramatic tension, but they remain within the influence of the now established mode. Style and matter move together in perfect accord to the horrible climax.

Lawrence stops short of the actual thrust which is to wrest mastery from the white man and give it to the Indian. Several reasons can be suggested why he does so. The climax is an abomination which Lawrence could not view with detachment. To let it happen would release a moral revulsion hitherto skillfully suppressed. Symbolically, it would be the destruction of mental consciousness, and there is no way of communicating such destruction by means that are dependent on mental consciousness, no matter how brilliantly language has been used to take the reader to its very brink. But perhaps the most compelling reason is in the nature of the style itself, which seeks to avoid the final, the isolated, and the absolute. The climax of the story would have been its own annihilation, or conversion into something quite different. (The only other way of reaching a conclusion would have been by a second process of gradual transmutation, which in the nature of the material was not possible.) Unsatisfactory though the ending may be because it leaves the reader gasping in an impossibly rarefied air, it is the only one that can be imagined for such a tale as this.

VII   *"Sun," "None of That," "Things," and "The Man Who Loved Islands"*

"The Woman Who Rode Away" appeared to have been written by the end of September, 1924, although the volume to which it gives its title did not appear until 1928. The kind of experiment which it represents is not followed up in the tales of the last six years of Lawrence's life, except for "Sun" (privately printed in 1926) and "The Escaped Cock"—though the latter is virtually a new departure, paralleled only in the verse of "The Ship of Death."

In "Sun" there is again the theme of a journey and a transformation. Julie's Italian sun cure "was not just taking sunbaths. It was much more than that. Something deep inside her unfolded and relaxed, and she was given. By some mysterious power inside her, deeper than her known consciousness and will, she was put into connection with the sun, and the stream flowed of itself, from her womb." The description of her sunbathing parallels sexual activity, or rather the quiescent, nonfrictional ecstasy which Lawrence, particularly in his later work, regards as the true and essentially feminine experience of sex. Unfortunately, the latter part of the story fails to realize Lawrence's intention. The sun turns Julie into a brassily insensitive creature, and one's sympathies inevitably go out to her kind, hesitant husband.

The other stories belonging to the later years are mostly reworkings of previous themes. "None of That" combines the satirical presentation of a new, independent woman—as in "The Princess"—with the pronouncedly sadistic streak of "The Border

Line." Cuesta, the bullfighter, is one of Lawrence's uneducated males with great animal magnetism, but here recognized by the narrator for the disgustingly bestial creature that he is.

"The Man Who Loved Islands" and "Things" (both 1928) are satirical tales, somewhat akin to "Two Blue Birds" and "Jimmy and the Desperate Woman," but much better done. "Things" shows Lawrence's mockingly colloquial style at its best. A particularly effective detail is the recurrent use of the image of a vine. It characterizes the idealist's need to cling to something: "there is a certain waving of loose ends upon the air, like the waving, yearning tendrils of the vine that spread and rotate, seeking something to clutch, something up which to climb towards the necessary sun."

"The Man Who Loved Islands" is a longer tale; divided into three sections, these correspond to the three islands on which the man lives. On the first he sets up an idyllic community, with himself as master. (Compton Mackenzie was the butt of this satire, but it is hard to believe that Lawrence was not also mocking at his own Utopian schemes for setting up an isolated community, with himself most certainly as the master.) After a while the attempt comes to grief, partly through natural human discord, partly because it proves too expensive, but also, Lawrence suggests, because the cruel and violent past of the island, which the man senses at certain times, but strives to ignore, curiously and damagingly reasserts itself. On the second island a smaller group, more like a family, is set up. This breaks up when the man has an affair with his housekeeper's daughter. It is "the automatism of sex" which he feels, not "true, delicate desire." He escapes to a third, minute, barren island where he becomes a pathetically absurd misanthropist, like Gulliver newly returned from the Houyhnhnms.

Finally, he is cut off and defeated by the snow and the sea, at a time when he knows that on the mainland it is summer "and the time of leaves." This ultimate isolation is reminiscent of Gerald's death in the snow of the Alps, though the tale has, of course, none of the strength of *Women in Love*. It is a satirical exposure of escapism and humanitarian illusion. Lawrence himself is not misanthropic in this tale, but he scores a telling point in making his islander set out as a genial, benevolent despot of his self-created community, only to end up as a neurotic despiser of mankind. His misanthropy is inherent in the illusions about man and nature with which he began.

VIII *"Mother" Tales and "The Virgin and the Gipsy"*

"The Lovely Lady," "Mother and Daughter," "The Rocking Horse Winner," and "The Virgin and the Gipsy" are all connected by the revival of Lawrence's early interest in the dominant mother figure. In "The Lovely Lady" an old woman contrives to retain her youthful sparkle and radiance by battening upon her son, as the grandmother in "The Virgin and the Gipsy" sits like a toad sucking in the life of the young people to feed her own. The theme throws one back to *Sons and Lovers,* but without the passionate sympathy for the mother. Only a sourly disenchanted view of motherhood remains—though, to be fair to Lawrence, what these tales convey is a detestation of the abuse of maternal power, not of motherhood generally.

In "The Rocking Horse Winner" the mother is thought by outsiders to be deeply devoted to her children, but she has no real love for them and only keeps up a pretense of affection. The boy who rocks himself to death in order to find winners, and so silence the voice that keeps saying "there must be more money," does so in an effort to put his relationship with his mother right. The mother obsession from which he suffers is of an unusual kind; it results from the lack of a "blood" connection which is overcompensated for by the child, rather than from a connection that is overemphasized by the mother. But the difference is not fundamental, for in both cases the natural flow from mother *to* child is perverted into an absorbing of life by the mother *from* the child.

The name of the Saywell family in "The Virgin and the Gipsy" indicates that respectable appearance covering a corrupt reality which is touched upon in the opening paragraph of "The Rocking Horse Winner." The rector has "a certain furtive self-righteousness." His continuing regard for the wife who has deserted him is worse than straightforward resentment, for it preserves a falsely idealized version of "She-who-was-Cynthia" as a "white snow-flower," pure and unsmirched, while her present reality silently accumulates all the horrors of the unmentionable. He himself slips back under the domination of the Mater—"one of those physically vulgar, clever old bodies who had got her own way all her life by buttering the weaknesses of her menfolk"

—who pretends to revere the rector's love for the idealized Cynthia while firmly establishing herself in the delinquent wife's place. And attending on the Mater is the embittered old maid, Aunt Cissie, who is subject to "strange green flares of rage" which betray her envy of "all young things" in whom life is strong.

Opposed to these are the rector's young daughters, Lucille and Yvette, who are recreations of Mary and Louisa in "Daughters of the Vicar"—except that Yvette is less responsible and practical than Louisa. Lawrence's rather simple antithesis between the older and the younger generations leads to some confusion of genres. The surface of the tale suggests a novel, recording accurate impressions of people, place, and tone of voice; but the sharp distinction between good and evil is that of a moral fable.

Yvette particularly suffers from this confusion. Her adolescent and feminine waywardness, her impudent naïveté are beautifully caught; and, when placed in relation to her father's affectionate indulgence, qualified by clerical respectability, they present a memorable realization of a father-daughter relationship. But Lawrence is not content with that. Yvette must be understood to embody a certain vital innocence which is puzzled, though not defenseless, in the face of the Saywell values. When the rector rebukes her for forming a friendship with an adulterous couple, his words are extravagant (he talks of "certain tendencies" which "end in criminal lunacy, unless they are curbed in time"), and they are matched by the extravagance of Lawrence's commentary ("Somewhere in his mind he was thinking unspeakable depravities about his daughter. . . . He was powerless against the lowest insinuations of his own mind"). This puts an enormous moral weight on the scene and on the characters of the rector and Yvette, one which they are hardly strong enough to carry. The rector is certainly a rather unpleasant figure, but he does not really appear in the story as the monster which he is here made out to be. Likewise, Yvette is attractive enough as a young woman of "heedless candour" and airy charm, despite a rather annoying manner of condescension to the world in general (she is a descendant of Gudrun in this respect); but as the embodiment of some mysterious moral superiority which "places" the rector—makes him feel "the slave's collar over his neck, finally"— she is overplayed. The Yvette that Lawrence has actually created is a less extraordinary person.

Lawrence's intention is to present Yvette as a natural aristocrat in whom there is a dimension that can be perceived only by another such natural aristocrat—in this instance, the gypsy. Ordinary mortals like her young suitor, Leo, touch only her surface, but the eyes of the gypsy "seemed to shoot her in some vital, undiscovered place, unerring." He has the power to stir her unconscious depths and so make her whole like an opened flower: "On her face was that tender look of sleep, which a nodding flower has when it is full out. Like a mysterious early flower, she was full out, like a snowdrop which spreads its three white wings in a flight into the waking sleep of its brief blossoming. The waking sleep of her full-opened virginity, entranced like snowdrop in the sunshine, was upon her."

The prose, however, is not distinguished. The contrast between the snowdrop image and the "white snow-flower" of the rector's arrested illusion of Cynthia indicates Lawrence's intention, but the lack of real command of the experience is betrayed in the striving for effect. One has only to recall how convincingly the supremacy of the unconscious stream of life over conscious divisions is expressed in "The Fox" to appreciate how inferior this story is to Lawrence's own best.

But, like Yvette, the gypsy is an interesting human being. Lawrence has caught the pride and suppressed contempt of a man belonging to an outcast race, and he has made the practical details of the gypsy way of life real enough to save the man from seeming to be spirited out of romantic literary gypsydom. Although the tale includes the expected fortune-telling that enshrines would-be truths, this does not come from the gypsy himself; and, in any case, it is not allowed to acquire the deplorably hocus-pocus character of Lewis' Celtic wisdom in "St. Mawr." Best of all, the gypsy's relations with Yvette are based upon mutual warmth of feeling. If she falls under his spell, he exercises no violating compulsion upon her. In this respect their relationship suggests that of Connie and Mellors rather than that of March and Henry or of Kate and Cipriano. They *enjoy* one another's company. The gypsy's saving Yvette from the flood is a natural climax to this relationship, in which he rescues her from a real danger, at great risk to himself, and in which symbolic overtones, though they certainly exist and are important, take second place to the simple physical realities of cold and wet and the gypsy's embracing of Yvette to restore her to life and warmth.

The result is that, for all its weaknesses, "The Virgin and the Gipsy" leaves an impression of simple, basic humanity—of which the gypsy's final "little letter, dated from some unknown place" (and signed with his own name, now revealed for the first time) is a fitting example.

IX "The Escaped Cock"

This renewal of humanity, already discussed in connection with *Lady Chatterley's Lover*, is the most distinctive quality of Lawrence's latest work. In general one cannot claim that he recovers the wonderful creative energy of his finest work in the period just before and during the first years of World War I. But there is a notable rise in the quality of his work, and a new serenity, quite different from the jeering bitterness which afflicts much of his writing in the early 1920s, appears. The most satisfying, and the most original, product of this Indian summer in Lawrence's creative life is undoubtedly "The Escaped Cock," apparently written in the spring of 1927.

Earl Brewster tells how he and Lawrence when on a tour in Italy saw a shop-window display of a toy white rooster escaping from an egg and how he remarked to Lawrence that it suggested a title, "The Escaped Cock—a Story of the Resurrection." In a letter to Brewster of May 3, 1927, Lawrence writes: "I wrote a story of the Resurrection, where Jesus gets up and feels very sick about everything, and can't stand the old crowd any more—so cuts out—and as he heals up, he begins to find what an astonishing place the phenomenal world is, far more marvellous than any salvation or heaven—and thanks his stars he needn't have a 'mission' any more. It's called *The Escaped Cock*, from that toy in Volterra."

Lawrence, who begins the tale with the cock, emphasizes from the beginning its perky vitality. A "shabby little thing" at first, it soon becomes "a dandy rooster," a "saucy, flamboyant bird, that has already made the final acquaintance of the three tattered hens," and has "a special fiery colour" to its crow. It is so lively that the peasant to whom it belongs has to tie it by the leg; but one morning, just before dawn, it snaps the string and escapes: "He gave a wild strange squawk, rose in one lift to the top of the wall, and there he crowed a loud and splitting crow. So loud, it woke the peasant."

The next sentence runs: "At the same time, at the same hour

before dawn, on the same morning, a man woke from a long sleep in which he was tied up." At this point one realizes that the account of the cock has been a prelude to the real tale; it is in a slightly different key from that in which the main tale is to proceed, and it has something of the effect of an elaborate simile. The humorously admiring description of the cock gives way to a more restrained style; and, as it dawns upon the reader that the "man" is the crucified Christ, it becomes apparent that this change of tone is due to the religious seriousness of the tale.

The point needs making with some delicacy. Lawrence does not move into a piously pseudobiblical style, though he does, in fact, make use throughout the tale of a slightly archaic diction and of a loosely coordinate syntax, frequently connecting with "And," which is undoubtedly reminiscent of the Bible. The clear, particularized realism and the colloquial easiness of the prelude continue into the main story, but they are modified in accordance with a natural sense of decorum which involves no rigid division between, say, the comically familiar style and the devotionally exalted. Lawrence's distinction is more subtle; it allows (and it is essential for his purpose that it should) a transition to be made which does not destroy the connection between the cock and the man. The cock's vigor and the instinctive pleasure it takes in its own world are a real parallel to what the resurrected man is to discover about the human world. And the two worlds (it is again part of the tale's meaning) are to be seen as belonging to the same larger world.

This last point is effectively symbolized in the meeting of the man who has just escaped from the tomb with the cock which has escaped from its tether. Following the road that leads away from the town, the man sees "The world, the same as ever, the natural world, thronging with greenness, a nightingale winsomely, wistfully, coaxingly calling from the bushes beside a runnel of water, in the world, the natural world of morning and evening, forever undying, from which he had died."

It is out of this "greenness," in a riot of color, that the bird comes—"the black and orange cock with the red comb, his tail-feathers streaming lustrous"—and the contrastingly white-clad man opens his "great white wings of a shroud" to catch it. When the peasant retrieves his cock, he gives hospitality to the man. But though the cock is tied again it still crows defiantly, and in its crow the man finds an emblem of the vast creative urge of life which is to him a revelation of the strong affirmative purpose of nature.

Along with this new understanding goes a repudiation of his didactic purpose. He sees his previous life as one which, dedicated to the whole of mankind, had left his own single being unrealized, and now he comes to a new kind of self-knowledge ("now I know my own limits"). "Self-importance"—which he associates with his "public life" of teaching and his mission of dying for mankind—gives way to an awareness of his hitherto neglected body: "For my reach ends in my finger-tips, and my stride is no longer than the ends of my toes. Yet I would embrace multitudes, I who have never truly embraced even one."

The man's new affirmative purpose does not, however, have the "ringing, defiant" quality of the cock. There is in it—and this is a new thing for Lawrence, too—a quieter, more serene quality that is almost classical in its avoidance of excess. In his encounter with Madeleine the man meets again the ecstatic self-denial of his previous religion of salvation. To her he is, or she would like him to be, the risen Messiah: but to the man excess in any form is objectionable. He regards Madeleine's repentance as being embraced with the same extravagance as was her former life of prostitution. "And I, in my mission," he says, "I too ran to excess." Now he renounces all attempts at preaching and proselytizing since they breed only violence such as that of his own crucifixion. In his present soothing, convalescent mood he prefers to be "purely alone" and to become at one with the "sun and the subtle salve of spring."

The serenity of the new mood is communicated in the wonderful description of a Mediterranean landscape which opens Part II. This introduces, in an appropriate context, the priestess of Isis. Instead of the vivid black, orange, and red of the cock, this passage is presented in the quieter colors of gold, yellow, white, and silver. The coastline is secluded, too, and the temple villa even more secluded. Its purity is broken into by the sordid incident of the slave who beats a girl slave and then copulates with her. But the effect of this incident is not to shatter the temple idyll. Rather, it keeps it in touch with the meanness that continues as an irreducible part of human existence. (Its counterpart in the first section of the tale is the slightly furtive anxiety and cupidity of the otherwise charitable peasant who gives shelter to the man who died.) And this meanness enters into the action of the tale, too, when the slave reports the man as an escaped malefactor and when the Roman overseer, at the end, tries to capture him by stealth. The escapism which is satirized in "The Man Who Loved Islands" as an ultimately dangerous illusion is avoided in "The Escaped Cock." The man is reborn into an awareness of the phenomenal world, not into an illusion that it is perfect and beautiful and innocent.

It is only Lawrence's natural aristocrats who transcend the meanness. Where Ursula and Gudrun and Yvette are concerned, the meanness is transcended only to let in a rather aggressive self-conceit; but the priestess, their descendant in this tale, is created in the same quiescent mood as the landscape to which she belongs. She is the daughter of a man who had fought with Antony against Octavius, and, when she was young, she had known both. She had shrunk from Caesar's "eagle-like rapacity," and, although "the golden Anthony had sat with her many a half-hour, in the splendour of his great limbs and glowing manhood" (the opposition between these two Lawrence obviously learned from Shakespeare), he recognizes that she is a flower "cool within," not a Cleopatra to his male glory.

The priestess is in the service of Isis in Search: of Isis seeking for the dismembered body of Osiris to make it whole and alive again so that he can embrace her and fertilize her womb. The application of this myth to the man who died is evident enough. His sleeping with the priestess completes his rediscovery of the body and leads to her becoming pregnant. Their actual consummation is a natural development of the tale. Its quality is important. It must be in keeping with the quiet non-excessive mood of the tale and with the priestess' lotus symbolism. Lawrence successfully achieves this by avoiding the full explicitness of *Lady Chatterley's Lover* (that is right for that novel, but would be disastrously out of place in this tale), and by resorting to the theme of "touch" poetically transformed so that it unites the sexual union of the lovers with the whole physical world renewed in the man's new physical awareness.

As in *Lady Chatterley's Lover,* the sexual activity is not allowed to acquire the illusion of permanency. The relationship which it seals is permanent, but sex itself is subject to the natural processes of change. This is, in fact, better expressed in "The Escaped Cock," partly because the sexual meeting of the priestess and the man is more clearly the culmination of a whole process of renewal, and partly because the poetic texture of the writing achieves a more organic connection between the human and the natural, like that which is realized in the imagery and rhythms of "The Ship of Death." "Touch" and the seasonal change are fused, and the fusion brings about a natural sense of the imminence of departure: "Plum-blossom blew from the trees, the time of the narcissus was past, anemones lit up the ground and were gone, the perfume of bean-field was in the air. All changed, the blossom of the universe changed its petals and swung round to look another way. The spring was fulfilled, a contact was established, the man and the woman were fulfilled of one another, and departure was in the air."

"The Escaped Cock" thus has a satisfying completeness. Its ending comes about as the natural fulfilling of the rhythm established within the tale. One has no sense of anything being forced or wrenched to bring it to a conclusion. As a "poem in prose," it suggests comparison with "The Woman Who Rode Away," but the comparison also suggests a world of difference, which is nowhere more striking than in their respective conclusions. While "The Woman Who Rode Away" poises the reader almost hysterically on the brink of an intolerable act of violence— a catastrophic end to a journey—"The Escaped Cock" ends with the rounding off of a natural seasonal movement and with the quiet pushing out of a boat from the shore.

CHAPTER 8

The Poems

LAWRENCE'S poems have been described as "acutely autobio-graphical." [1] This is obviously true of his earlier *Rhyming Poems* and *Look! We Have Come Through!* which concern such private matters as the love affairs with "Miriam" and with "Helen," his feelings about schoolteaching, and his elopement with Frieda. This statement is less applicable, however, to the satirical *Pansies* and *Nettles*, and scarcely at all to the best of Lawrence's poems—*Birds, Beasts and Flowers* and *Last Poems*—which are autobiographical only in the sense that they reflect his highly idiosyncratic point of view. The term is, therefore, mis-leading; it does not allow for the different kinds of material to be found in the poetry. "Personal," which has greater breadth of meaning, is a better word; and it also has the merit of suggesting an important truth about the way the poems are written.

Lawrence did not regard himself as a traditional poet writing poems of "exquisite finality, perfection which belongs to all that is far off," but as the poet of "the immediate present." [2] His most characteristic poems are

> *substance itself, that flows in thick*
> *flame of flesh forever travelling*
> *like the flame of a candle, slow and quick*
> *fluttering and softly unravelling.*
> ("The Risen Lord")

They are not carelessly written. In a brilliant but perverse essay, R. P. Blackmur has sought to prove that Lawrence had no inter-est in the technique of poetry and that this lack ruined him as a poet. [3] The existence of four different versions of "Bavarian Gentians," for example, and the overlapping of various poems, which suggest repeated attempts to express the same theme, provide factual evidence to disprove this criticism. Lawrence's poems are of very unequal quality, and his mastery of the special kind of technique which they display comes only gradually and even then only at fortunate moments. But, when it is completely his, the poems have a fluid, responsive quality that makes them seem emanations of his personality rather than "artifices of eternity."[4]

I *The Early Poems:* Pansies *and* Nettles

Lawrence himself comments on the earlier poems: "They were struggling to say something which it takes a man twenty years to be able to say. . . . A young man is afraid of his demon and puts his hand over the demon's mouth sometimes and speaks for him. And the things the young man says are very rarely poetry."[5] The sort of poem that the young man wrote can be seen in "Michael Angelo." The desire to impress is betrayed in a self-conscious literary style, which also emphasizes to the poem's detriment the heavy indebtedness to Blake's "Tiger":

> *Who shook thy roundness in his finger's cup?*
> *Who sunk his hands in firmness down thy sides*
> *And drew the circle of his grasp, O man,*
> *Along thy limbs delighted as a Bride's?*

The use of rhyme is embarrassing. In very few of his poems ("Giorno dei Morti" is a notable exception) does Lawrence make good use of rhyme. Its clinching effect is an impediment to the fluidity that his personal vision demands, and its failure in such poems as "Michael Angelo" is evidence, not, as Blackmur implies, that Lawrence should have persevered with traditional form, but that his abandonment of rhyme in the later verse was right for him.

The early poems are in general marred by artificiality both in diction and form, but the true Lawrentian note is often heard, if not sustained, especially in poems dealing with the three main themes of Love, Nature, and the mother-son relationship. In "Monologue of a Mother," expressing a mother's feeling of despair at being deserted by her son, the literary weakness typical of the early verse is very noticeable, and there is also a serious failure to project the mother dramatically. But the son's emotions are effectively communicated. In the image of "a thin white bird blown out of the northern seas" into the "sooty garden," the industrial ugliness of Lawrence's own home combines with his inheritance of nineteenth-century Romanticism to provide a symbol of the emotionally crippling effect of the mother's possessiveness that is both lucid and unforced.

A fuller treatment of the mother-son relationship is given in "End of Another Home Holiday." Nature is drawn into and made part of the personal conflict. The mother's possessiveness (the more difficult for the son to resist because she is "lonely, greying now") is contrasted with the undemanding cycle of Nature:

> *The sun and the rain do not ask the secret*
> *Of the time when the grain struggles down in the dark.*
> *The moon walks her lonely way without anguish,*
> *Because no one grieves over her departure.*

The son is distressed not only because he is causing his mother pain but because he is in an unnatural situation which makes the filial relationship a barrier to his own development. The experience is essentially that of an adolescent, and its quality of immaturity is faithfully reflected by the poising of the poem in the twilight region between impressionism and youthful didacticism.

The conflict in "End of Another Home Holiday" presupposes a close bond between Man and Nature. For Lawrence, human life was simply an extension of the life of Nature, and it was, therefore, subject to the same laws and penalties. His use of the pathetic fallacy is the technical means by which he suggests this concept. In "The Wild Common," for example, it is used to unite the poet and the rabbits that he sees on the common by an almost physical bond:

> *Are they asleep?—are they living?—Now see, when I*
> *Lift my arms, the hill bursts and heaves under their spurting kick!*

It is also the means by which Lawrence conveys the interaction of the human and the natural in love. The reactions of the swallow, the waterhen, and the rabbit in "Love on the Farm" to the man's approach are made to anticipate the woman's horror at her lover's brutality, and in this way the existence of an extremely close bond between her and the rest of Nature is suggested. The device is, in fact, made to serve this purpose a little too obviously when the woman feels as if caught in a snare by her lover: "I know not what fine wire is round my throat."

In "Snap-Dragon" the pathetic fallacy is used to explore the psychology of love. The symbolic method of this poem, as Harry T. Moore says, is akin to that of novels like *The Rainbow* and *Women in Love;* but it is not, therefore, "less important in the study of the development of Lawrence's poetry."[6] On the contrary, the repetitive and chameleonlike use of symbols is an important step towards the repetition, with deepening and widening significance, which becomes the technique of "Snake" and "Bavarian Gentians." The central image is that of the snapdragon itself which puts out its "tongue" when squeezed, and this is also a phallic image in which the human and the natural combine. Lawrence contrives a language which enables him to speak of the external natural and internal human worlds at the same time, and he supports this effect by the repetition and transmutation of symbols so that the same influence is felt to be at work in different contexts. The image of the "cup" in the second line recurs later as "My Grail, a brown bowl twined/With swollen veins that met in the wrist"—with the difference that it refers now to the girl's hand as she squeezes the snapdragon. Similarly, the image of the girl as "a settling bird" in the third stanza later becomes "a brown bird," symbolic of passions, and it not to be completely separated from the image of the intruder cuckoo. This use of imagery helps the different parts of the poem to fuse, and it also emphasizes the unity of the human and the natural.

Most of the poems in *Look! We Have Come Through!* are not yet artistically mature, but they are a remarkable advance towards poetic honesty. The verse is more Whitmanesque than that of the earlier work, and the material is more blatantly didactic and doctrinal. The fact that these poems belong to the period when Lawrence was still developing his ideas about love and marriage is evident in a certain stridency and even crudeness of statement. Many of them read like entries in a journal or notebook. There is the occasional poem, however, in which the pressure of the demon leads, not to the neglect of form, but to the creation of a new form appropriate to the thing that is being urged into expression. "Bei Hennef" is such a poem. The experience which it records is transient, and the form is a true medium for this because it aims not at a studied completeness, but at capturing the ebb and flow of feeling. It is a form uniquely suited to the expression of Lawrence's belief in the supreme importance of "the magnificent here and now of life in the flesh."

There are certain lines in "Bei Hennef" which, taken out of their context, would seem overemphatic, but which really belong to the confidence and exaltation of one particular time and place. That moment is created in the first half dozen lines; the rest of the poem is the "thought" arising from this moment. Words like "twittering" and "flickers" reinforce this impression, as do the short sentences colloquially linked by "And"; the occasional omission of a verb in an exclamation; the observance of normal prose order; and the casually unfinished "What more—?" Such didacticism as creeps into the poem in the fifth stanza is corrected by the final self-reminder, "Strange, how we suffer in spite of this!" This comment brings us back to the fact of transience once more.

The immediacy and the freshness achieved by this technique make even the flimsiest of Lawrence's poems after *Look! We Have Come Through!* highly readable. *Pansies* and *Nettles*, though for the most part written without great care, always have this redeeming freshness. Many of the poems in these two collections ("True Democracy," "Nottingham's New University," "Don'ts," "Innocent England") revert to rhyme; but Lawrence manages to combine with it the liberating technical advances made in *Look! We Have Come Through!* The resultant verse is both satirically pointed and casually mocking, providing an ideal medium for the expression of Lawrence's essentially working-class dislike of stuffiness and affectation. On the other hand, a poem like "The Oxford Voice" owes its success entirely to fluid rhythm and to sensitive use of varied line lengths with no assistance from rhyme; and such is Lawrence's virtuosity that he can even use this verse for epigram ("The Mosquito Knows").

According to Richard Aldington, *Pansies* "came out of Lawrence's nerves, and not out of his real self";[7] and Dallas Kenmare even suggests that the satirical part of *Last Poems* should have been suppressed.[8] Miss Kenmare's attitude to Lawrence is typical of a certain type of admirer. For her Lawrence was a great adventurer in the world of the imagination, but he was tragically mistaken in attempting to apply his vision to the world of fact. This may well be true of such schemes as Rananim, but it is a great pity if the thesis is allowed to obscure the practical side of Lawrence. He took great delight in haymaking, cooking, and even housework; and he was gifted with a good deal of straight-forward common sense which is an important aspect of his work as a writer. Not the least valuable thing about *Pansies*, *More Pansies*, and *Nettles* is that they make it impossible to forget this practical side of Lawrence, and they insure that we do not overlook the grasp of everyday reality shown in the great poems.

II Birds, Beasts and Flowers

As a poet Lawrence belongs to the Romantic tradition, but he also relates that tradition to what is familiar and commonplace. The wonderfully sinuous, incantatory quality of his mature free verse is a new triumph of Romanticism:

> *He drank enough*
> *And lifted his head, dreamily, as one who has drunken,*
> *And flickered his tongue like a forked night on the air, so black;*
> *Seeming to lick his lips,*
> *And looked around like a god, unseeing, into the air,*
> *And slowly turned his head,*
> *And slowly, very slowly, as if thrice adream,*
> *Proceeded to draw his slow length curving round*
> *And climb again the broken bank of my wall-face.*
>
> ("Snake")

But even in this verse everyday reality is suggested by the "broken bank" and the colloquialism of "Seeming to lick his lips"; and elsewhere in "Snake" everyday reality is yet more prominent. Lawrence's method is to counterpoint the two different levels of experience. The three plain prosaic lines of the opening ("I in my pyjamas for the heat" even a little com-ically familiar) form a contrast with the "deep, strange-scented shade of the great dark carob-tree" of the fourth line. As the poem grows, this contrast is enlarged into one between the voices of the poet's "accursed human education" and the mysterious in-junctions of "one of the lords/Of life." Undoubtedly, there is a didactic element in this poem; but—as in "Bei Hennef"—it is the didacticism of a particular moment which is created with a most skillfully persuasive impressionism. The contrast swells naturally into significance, aided by the repetitive, transmuting

technique learned in the earlier poems. The repetition is partly
hypnotic, but it is also a way of drawing the reader into a deepening vortex of meaning that swirls him down from the prosaic
surface to unconscious depths: "earth-brown, earth-golden from
the burning bowels of the earth."

More subtle in effect are the repetitions that occur at longer
intervals. Thus, "flickered his two-forked tongue from his lips"
is at first a purely descriptive detail. When it is repeated, in the
incantatory passage quoted above, "forked" applies to night,
making the snake and the night seem part of the same force and
adding depth to the antithesis that runs throughout the poem
between darkness and the brightness of "the intense still noon."
The words "night" and "black" recall the statement that "in
Sicily the black, black snakes are innocent, the gold are ven-
omous." But now the association of the words "right" and "black"
with the snake's looking "around like a god" subtly alters the
significance of this statement. The snake of the poem is "gold,"
but, paradoxically, also "black" because of its association with the
true, potent "innocence" of darkness, which is not the same as
the mere harmlessness that "human education" approvingly
calls "innocent." "Night" and "black" also reach forward to "the
black hole, the earth-lipped fissure in the wall-front," a phrase
which itself began as "a fissure in the earth-wall," then changed
to "the dark door of the secret earth," and now combines with
the mysterious darkness of the snake in the compound "earth-
lipped."

In *Birds, Beasts and Flowers* there are three main types of
poem: (1) poems of simple impressionism such as "Mosquito,"
"Peach," the two bat poems, and "Baby Tortoise"; (2) impressionist poems which, like "Snake," move towards symbolism
but are not strictly symbolic (other examples are "Figs," "Grapes,"
"Fish," and "Turkey-Cock"); (3) poems that are symbolic from
the start, such as "Cypresses," "Humming-Bird," and the four
"Evangelistic Beasts." In the poems of the first kind, the flexibility of Lawrence's mature free verse is used simply to reflect, as faithfully as possible, the essential life of the subject,
or to record with seismographic delicacy the feelings which it
arouses in the poet. They are full of vivid descriptive phrases, such
as "Swallows with spools of dark thread sewing the shadows together" ("Bat") and "shallow-silvery wine-glass on a short stem"

("Peach"); and they also reveal a delightful sense of humor which is strikingly different from the acid bitterness of *Pansies* and *Nettles*.

The second group has already been illustrated by the analysis of "Snake." Not all of the poems in this group are equally successful in transforming impressionism into symbolism, nor do they have the same significance. "Grapes," "Fish," and "Kangaroo" evoke the same mythological suggestions as "Snake," but "Bare Fig-Trees" and "Elephant" are political. These poems tend to become vigorous pamphleteering; they make a point effectively, but lack the originality of the mythological poems. What is missing is the intuitive penetration that enables Lawrence to give a necessarily subjective description of nonhuman life a seemingly objective quality. In "Fish" the sheer otherness of fish life is wonderfully conveyed:

> *Your life a sluice of sensation along your sides,*
> *A flush at the flails of your fins, down the whorl of your tail,*
> *And water wetly on fire in the grates of your gills,*
> *Fixed water-eyes.*

The wit of this poem is also remarkable. It achieves a subtle mockery of animal sexuality by humorously emphasizing the contrast between the sex lives of fish and animals; it is at once profoundly sympathetic and profoundly ironical.

In the best of the poems belonging to the third group, although experience is subjected from the beginning to a conscious purpose, the symbolism remains capable of the resonant effect which it has in poems of the second group. "Humming-Bird," for example, evokes an image of primitive hummingbirds which is at the same time presented as a consciously purposeful symbol. The most remarkable poems of this kind are the four "Evangelistic Beasts." They differ from the rest of *Birds, Beasts and Flowers* in that their subjects have a symbolic significance apart from that given them by Lawrence; the tension between the old and the new meanings is used for satiric effect. In "St. Luke" Lawrence's bull is a creature of dark sexual energy, baffled and frustrated by Christianity. The technique by which this is expressed is akin to that of the impressionist poems, but the repetition is emphatic, not cumulative, and straightforward assertion is added to the impressionism. The technique of "St. Mark," on the other hand, is nearer to that of *Pansies*. It is mockingly colloquial, as befits the description of a lion which has been converted to a curly sheep dog with a few remaining "dangerous propensities." Both poems are attacks on the denial of "sensuality" which accompanies Christianity, and their different methods enable Lawrence to stress different aspects: in "St. Luke" the frustration and in "St. Mark" the enervation of natural animal vigor. Yet both succeed in presenting the beasts as beasts, not merely as satirical emblems.

III Last Poems

Lawrence's poetry is at once highly diverse and highly unified. The same qualities and the same ideas recur in widely different contexts. But, if there is much overlapping, there is comparatively little mere duplication. The capacity for change is characteristic of both man and his work. He was always striving to break new ground. Even the approach of death was treated not as a culmination of his work, or as a time to "fashion his soul"[9] by the contemplation of Platonic abstractions, but as a part of a continuous process of discovery.

The great theme of *Last Poems* is Lawrence's inner struggle to understand and accept death. As stated in the title of one of the poems, "Death is Not Evil, Evil is Mechanical." Death is the equipoise of Life, making renewal possible by destroying whatever is decayed and exhausted. Not only men but ideas and the civilizations based on them grow old and need to be destroyed in order to make way for new life. A moribund idea is a tyrannical inhibitor of life, as Lawrence believed Christianity to be in the twentieth century. With the destruction of the outworn civilization, the time comes for the birth of a new one; or, in accordance with a cycle not unlike that of Spenser's Garden of Adonis, for the rebirth of an old one that has been refreshed by its absence from earth.

This rebirth is hailed in such poems as "The Greeks are Coming," "The Argonauts," "Middle of the World," and "For the Heroes are dipped in Scarlet." In these poems the present and the past (which, however, with Lawrence is also the implicit future) are ironically juxtaposed. In "The Greeks are Coming" the ancient ships of Knossos are contrasted with the ocean liner "leaving a long thread of dark smoke/like a bad smell. . . ." In "Middle of the World" the mythical "slim black ship of Dionysos" comes "sailing in/with grape-vines up the mast, and dolphins leaping. . . ." These ships contrast with "the smoking ships/of the P. & O. and the Orient Line and all the other stinkers."

The myth-making in these poems is an expanded symbolism expressing the life-assertive civilization that is due to take the place of the present Christian-Platonic one. The opening lines of "For the Heroes are dipped in Scarlet" have direct reference to this idea: "Before Plato told the great lie of ideals/men slimly went like fishes, and didn't care." These are the men of the past who are now to become the heroes of the future. The explanation of their scarlet color is to be found in *Etruscan Places;* "Man all scarlet was his bodily godly self,"[10] and in *Apocalypse* "the heroes and the hero-kings glowed in the face red as poppies that the sun shines through. It was the colour of glory: it was the colour of the wild bright blood, which was life itself."[11] Scarlet symbolizes their renewed vitality.

The heroes also have the feet of "moon-lit dancers" and the meaning of this reference to the moon is only apparent after a wider study of Lawrence's work. Some special personal significance in the moon for Lawrence undoubtedly influenced his use of it in his writing. It occurs in at least ten different poems, and in the earlier of these its significance is obscurely personal. In the later poems, however, a more specific meaning can be attached to it, the clue to which can again be found in *Apocalypse.* In this work the moon is described as a goddess who beneficently watches over the body but, when the body is outraged, turns into a destructive power. The sun also is both creative and destructive. In its destructive aspect it is a red lion, a symbol taken over in the later poems for the evil potency of modern civilization. Generally, the somewhat confusing duplication of aspects in *Apocalypse* is avoided in the poetry. The sun comes to be associated with the destructive phase in the Lawrentian cycle of death and rebirth; the moon, with the mysterious creative power that insures renewal. The plainest statement of this contrast is to be found in "The Hostile Sun" (printed with *More Pansies,* but clearly belonging with *Last Poems*); but poetically "Invocation to the Moon," "The Argonauts," and the fragmentary "Prayer" are superior.

The two finest poems in *Last Poems* are "Bavarian Gentians" and "The Ship of Death." In these two poems Lawrence carries his exploration of death to its poetically most satisfying conclusion. The opening of "Bavarian Gentians" is beautifully somber and assured. The long lines achieve a slow suggestive rhythm that vibrates on the unconscious, and assonance and alliteration give the whole poem music and fluidity of movement. The gentians are a torch guiding the poet into the regions of death, but no such crude statement is made in the poem. The descriptive and the mythological are fused in phrases like "the smoking blueness of Pluto's gloom," and the image of the torch increases its symbolic suggestiveness gradually through the transmuting effect of Lawrence's repetitive technique. It passes from being a "torch-flower of the blue-smoking darkness," lighting the pathway to Hades, to a nuptial torch, "shedding darkness on the lost bride and her groom" (Persephone and Pluto). Death is thus tacitly transformed from something merely destructive to something mysteriously destructive-creative, an effect which is further heightened by the paradoxical treatment throughout the poem of the gentians as flowers which are bright with darkness ("giving off darkness, blue darkness, as Demeter's pale lamps give off light").

In "The Ship of Death" the two basic images are the falling fruit of autumn and the little ship of death which takes its origin from "the little bronze ship of death," mentioned in *Etruscan Places*, that carries the dead Etruscan "over to the other world."[12] The clue to the poem's meaning is also to be found in *Etruscan Places*: to an Etruscan, death "was neither an ecstasy of bliss, a heaven, nor a purgatory of torment. It was just a natural continuance of the fullness of life. Everything was in terms of life, of living."[13] The recurrent autumnal imagery enables Lawrence to suggest this "natural continuance of the fullness of life" and to treat of decay without implying despair. The little ship makes it possible for him to emphasize the creativeness of death and to develop the idea of death, as not an end but as the start of a new journey. The vessel is described as "the fragile ship of courage, the ark of faith," though the dangerously rhetorical largeness of these phrases is also offset by the practical details in the lines immediately following: "with its store of food and little cooking pans/and change of clothes." And the journey itself, though it is towards a region of mysterious darkness, has a remarkably dramatic immediacy. The phrase "soundless, ungurgling flood" is a particularly good example of Lawrence's success in combining sensuous impact with evocative symbolism. This quality in the writing makes the whole journey both convincing and richly suggestive.

In the last two sections Lawrence's achievement is most impressive. He completely avoids the splendidly rhetorical in his treatment of rebirth. When the body steps from its little ship in "the cruel dawn of coming back to life," it has an almost convalescent delicacy:

> *The flood subsides, and the body, like a worn sea-shell*
>   *emerges strange and lovely.*
> *And the little ship wings home, faltering and lapsing*
>   *on the pink flood,*
> *and the frail soul steps out, into the house again*
>   *filling the heart with peace.*

This is a resurrection which involves no transcendence of time and mortality. It is more literally a rebirth than that of Christianity, yet part of an interpretation of life that is emphatically religious, finding its sense of the numinous in Nature rather than the supernatural. Death is as much a critical reality for Lawrence as it is for the orthodox Christian, but it is not for him the threshold of eternity and is not, therefore, a subject for apocalyptic fervor. Death is a part of natural life, a purifier that destroys the old and makes way for the new. But this does not make it easier to accept than the Christian view. It is still "the voyage of oblivion," the leap into the unknown which tests the faith of the religious man. The quality of Lawrence's response to this test can be seen in the poetry of "The Ship of Death" itself, and particularly in these last two sections. The simplicity and the quiet assurance with which they communicate his belief in the cycle of Nature and in the unity of the human and the natural reveal an achieved confidence and serenity.

CHAPTER 9

Reputation and Influence

I Lawrence and the Critics

WE MUST remember," wrote T. S. Eliot in 1935, "that what a writer does to people is not necessarily what he intends to do. It may be only what people are capable of having done to them. People exercise an unconscious selection in being influenced. A writer like D. H. Lawrence may be in his effect either beneficial or pernicious." [1] Open-ended as this statement appears to be, Eliot in fact regarded Lawrence's influence as pernicious rather than beneficial, and his reference to a writer's influence being limited to "what people are capable of having done to them" unwittingly explains the ground of his dislike. He and Lawrence were too different for either to be in sympathy with the other, at least during the 1920's, and, one imagines, if Lawrence had been alive, during the 1930's as well.

Eliot's own positions were so entrenched that he was incapable of responding to Lawrence freely and sympathetically. He could only fit him into a predetermined scheme. In an essay on "Le Roman Anglais Contemporain" published in *La Nouvelle Revue Francaise* in May, 1927, Eliot makes the astonishing statement that "L'oeuvre de M. Lawrence n'est jamais troublée par l'humeur, la gaîté ou le persiflage; aucune diversion politique, théologique ou artistique ne vient nous distraire." When Lawrence's characters make love, Eliot continues, "et ils ne font pas d'autre chose," they lose all the refinements which several centuries have elaborated to make love bearable. The attitude towards sex revealed in the last remark is one indication of the gulf between the two writers. Eliot, who is fond of applying the word "morbid" to Lawrence, is himself morbid about sex in his essay on Baudelaire; and it is not surprising that in *After Strange Gods* (1933) he should dismiss *Lady Chatterley's Lover* with flippant and superficial remarks: "Our old acquaintance, the game-keeper, turns up again: the social obsession which makes his well-born—or almost well-born—ladies offer themselves to—or make use of—plebeians springs from the same morbidity which makes other of his female characters bestow their favours upon savages. The author of that book seems to me to have been a very sick man indeed." [2]

After Strange Gods contains Eliot's fullest attack on Lawrence. It is "a primer of modern heresy" with Lawrence as the prime heretic. Eliot's theme is "the crippling effect upon men of letters, of not having been born and brought up in the environment of a living and central tradition." [3] The application of this theme to Lawrence has been refuted once and for all by F. R. Leavis in *D. H. Lawrence, Novelist*. Eliot was ignorant of the actual education that Lawrence had received and of the vitality of the provincial tradition in which he had been reared. But what is more interesting to note is the way in which Eliot sets up a false antithesis between the artist who is nourished and controlled by a living tradition and the artist, of whom he tries to make Lawrence an example, who is led only by the will o' the wisp of his own "inner light." Lawrence's advocacy of a rooted, not a rootless, individuality is ignored, as are the common sense and self-criticism which act as a constant check to extravagance.

The clash of personalities is obvious. Eliot distrusts himself and turns to external authority for support. Lawrence is conscious of society as a dead shell and is less in need of the support offered by an *ex cathedra* authority. Both are concerned with order, but one is driven by his own need to subscribe to an institutionalized form of order, the other to reject institutions as the betrayal of vital order and to seek for a harmonizing principle in the individual. [4]

Other famous contemporaries of Lawrence who passed judgment on his work include Henry James, Virginia Woolf, Arnold Bennett, and E. M. Forster. James loftily "trifled with the exordia" and dismissed Lawrence as hanging "in the dusty rear" of Gilbert Cannan, Hugh Walpole, and Compton Mackenzie. [5] Virginia Woolf wrote that Lawrence had "moments of greatness, but hours of something very different." Arnold Bennett, however, appreciated Lawrence's intentions ("He tried to fish up sex from the mud into which it has been sunk for several hypocritical and timid English generations past."); [6] and he recognized him for the great artist that he was. He also gave practical effect to his admiration for Lawrence by protesting over the suppression of *The*

Rainbow in 1915 and by anonymously giving Lawrence money through J. B. Pinker.

Forster also recognized Lawrence's distinction and spoke up for him. In *Aspects of the Novel* (1927) he groups Lawrence with Dostoevski, Melville, and Emily Brontë as a novelist of "prophecy"—the power which extends reality into an imaginative dimension. (As a concrete example of Lawrence's prophetic quality, he cites the scene in *Women in Love* where Birkin stones the moon's reflection.) Shortly after Lawrence's death, when even the obituarists were scant of praise, Forster risked his own reputation as a judge by claiming for Lawrence a position of preeminence among modern writers and by making an important critical point in asserting the impossibility of detaching Lawrence's art from his ideas: "He was both a preacher and a poet, and some people, myself included, do not sympathize with the preaching. Yet I feel that without the preaching, the poetry could not exist. With some writers one can disentangle the two, with him they are inseparable." [7]

The first book to be written on Lawrence came from the pen of an American, Herbert J. Seligmann. His *D. H. Lawrence, An American Interpretation* (1924) is at times hectically adjectival, and the author has an exaggerated respect for what were then Lawrence's most recent novels (*Aaron's Rod* and *Kangaroo*), but on *Sons and Lovers* and on *Women in Love* he is still very well worth reading. Seligmann ranges over all the various kinds of Lawrence's writings and notes several things which later critics were to miss. He is aware of the strong sense of humor behind Tom Brangwen's marriage speech in Chapter 5 of *The Rainbow* and of the presence of this humor in the short stories; moreover, he recognizes the quality of "the incandescent moment" in Lawrence's poetry. Particularly concerned with Lawrence's "message" for America, Seligmann emphasizes the challenge of his attacks on the leveling tendency of democracy; on the evils of mechanization; and on the rise of the independent, managing woman. *Studies in Classic American Literature* is hailed as containing "brilliantly written analyses" which are the "foundation for a new American critical literature"—a judgment which is essentially confirmed by Edmund Wilson who includes the whole of the *Studies* in his critical anthology, *The Shock of Recognition* (1943).

No studies of Lawrence were published in England during his

lifetime, but after his death in 1930 books appeared by Richard Aldington, Stephen Potter, and Rebecca West, and essays were published by Middleton Murry and F. R. Leavis. In 1931 Murry published his notorious *Son of Woman* which, like so many of the books produced by Lawrence's friends and ex-friends in the 1930's, reflected the author's personal involvement with Lawrence to the detriment of serious criticism. Murry, however, was a very distinguished literary critic, which most of the later memoirists were not; and his book is at least a genuine attempt to assess the significance of Lawrence. What spoils it is Murry's inability to get beyond the man—who had made such a disastrous impact upon him personally—to the essential artist. As Aldous Huxley says, in the Introduction to *The Letters of D. H. Lawrence* (1932); *Son of Woman* is "about a Lawrence whom you would never suspect, from reading that curious essay in destructive hagiography, of being an artist. . . . His book is *Hamlet* without the Prince of Denmark—for all its metaphysical subtleties and its Freudian ingenuities, very largely irrelevant." [8]

Huxley himself in this Introduction writes a fine appreciation of Lawrence. Like Forster, he stresses the visionary element in Lawrence's work and is the first to connect him with the Wordsworthian "unknown modes of being."

In his 1930 essay (reprinted with slight additions in *For Continuity*, 1933) Leavis, the greatest of Lawrence's critics, makes his first contribution to the understanding and assessment of Lawrence. He realizes the full seriousness of Lawrence's indictment of modern industrial society and perceives Lawrence's affinity with Blake in his "power of distinguishing his own feelings and emotions from conventional sentiment" and in his "terrifying honesty." [9] Many of the incidental comments and judgments, however, make strange reading today. Although Leavis describes *Sons and Lovers*, for example, as "a beautiful and poignant book, showing a sincerity in the record of emotional life such as is possible only to genius," he goes on to say that it is "difficult to get through." [10] And a similar charge is leveled at *Women in Love*. Even *The Rainbow* is found in its exploration of the "shifting tensions of the inner life" to produce an effect of "monotony." [11] *Lady Chatterley's Lover* shows "a narrowing down" compared with the earlier novels, but it is deemed an "artistic success." [12] And, most surprising judgment of all, *The Lost Girl* is Lawrence's "best *novel*." [13]

D. H. Lawrence, Novelist (1955), however, is the book in which Leavis delivers his considered assessment of Lawrence's work. *The Rainbow* and *Women in Love,* together with certain of the tales (notably "St. Mawr") now become the central corpus on which Leavis bases his claim, amply justified by close analysis, that "Lawrence is a great artist, a creative writer" and "one of the major novelists of the English tradition." [14] *Lady Chatterley's Lover* is downgraded for its "willed insistence" on the four-letter words. (More recently still, Leavis has made it clear that he does not share the high opinion currently held of this novel, but he has not produced a convincingly detailed adverse analysis to match the effectiveness of his recommendation of *The Rainbow* and of *Women in Love.*)

Leavis' early errors of judgment show the need for tolerance among critics, although Leavis himself has not been the quickest to learn this lesson. The substance of his contribution to Lawrentian criticism remains unimpaired, however; for it is to Leavis more than to any other one person that English readers are indebted not only for demonstration of Lawrence's achievement specifically as an artist but also for understanding of "the insight, the wisdom, the revived and re-educated feeling for health, that Lawrence brings." [15]

In the 1930's Lawrence's reputation, though growing, was not extensive; and comparatively little good criticism was published. The political preoccupations of the time did not favor attention to Lawrence, who was either superficially misread as a Fascist, or squeezed into the straitjacket of Marxist literary theory, as in Christopher Caudwell's essay, "D. H. Lawrence: A Study of the Bourgeois Artist" (published in *Studies in a Dying Culture,* 1938). Caudwell argues that Lawrence was "well aware of the fact that the pure artist cannot exist to-day, and that the artist must inevitably be a man hating cash relationships and the market, and profoundly interested in the relations between persons," but, says Caudwell, his solution was not to identify himself with the struggle of the working class, which, according to Marxist theory, he should have done, but to seek escape by a "return to the primitive." [16]

A more detached—and still very influential—essay devoted to Lawrence's poetry is R. P. Blackmur's "D. H. Lawrence and Expressive Form" (1935). Blackmur's criticism is based on preferences that suggest, and very likely derive from, T. S. Eliot; but

Blackmur is, nevertheless, very sympathetic to Lawrence's point of view. He deplores what he regards as the inadequate art which prevents Lawrence's "powerful sensibility" and "profound experience" from achieving an ordered framework and hence full communication. Because Lawrence's poetry lacks "the protection and support of a rational imagination," he has "left us the ruins of great intentions." [17]

Blackmur's argument is intelligent and subtle, but his criticism is perverse because he looks for what is not there, instead of patiently exploring what is. In this respect there is a sharp contrast between his approach to Lawrence's poetry and that of A. Alvarez in the best essay yet to have appeared on Lawrence's poetry "D. H. Lawrence, The Single State of Man" (*The Shaping Spirit*, 1958). Alvarez rejects the suggestion that Lawrence was a careless writer; and he cites the fact that Lawrence worked over his poems again and again. According to Alvarez, Lawrence had a genius for flowing flexibility which "can never be laid out into a system, for it comes instead from the poet's rigorous but open alertness. And so there is care, even discipline, but no formal perfection and finish." [18] This statement rings true to the poetry that one actually reads, as Blackmur's essay does not.

In 1939 W. Y. Tindall's *D. H. Lawrence and Susan His Cow* appeared. Tindall does Lawrence the honor of giving his sources careful, scholarly attention; but his criticism is spoiled by its tone of urbane condescension. Tindall's mockery reflects a state of affairs far more perilous for Lawrence's reputation than Blackmur's denial of his art; and, in fact, it ushers in a period of almost total neglect of Lawrence. Not until after World War II did Lawrence's reputation revive. Then the recovery was rapid; and, since 1950—the year in which Penguin Books in England published ten paperback volumes of Lawrence—criticism of his work has increased in quantity and some (but by no means all of it) in quality. The notable feature of postwar criticism is the amount which has poured from the universities. Lawrence, along with Joyce, Yeats, and Eliot, has become recognized as a major literary figure of the twentieth century.

The most interesting of the postwar studies of Lawrence (a somewhat larger number of them are published in America than in Britain) are: *Portrait of a Genius But. . . .* , by Richard Aldington (1950); *D. H. Lawrence and Human Existence,* by Father William Tiverton (1951); *The Achievement of D. H. Law-*

rence, an anthology of Lawrence criticism, edited by Harry T. Moore and F. J. Hoffman (1953); *The Intelligent Heart,* by Harry T. Moore (1955)—by far the best biography of Lawrence yet to have been written; *D. H. Lawrence, Novelist,* by F. R. Leavis (1955); *The Love Ethic of D. H. Lawrence,* by Mark Spilka (1955); *The Dark Sun,* by Graham Hough (1956); *D. H. Lawrence, A Composite Biography,* edited by Edward Nehls (1957-9)—three immensely valuable volumes gathering together extracts from memoirs; *A D. H. Lawrence Miscellany,* edited by Harry T. Moore (1959)—a second anthology; and *D. H. Lawrence: The failure and the triumph of art* by Eliseo Vivas (1960). In addition, various books by G. H. Bantock, Dorothy van Ghent, Arnold Kettle, William Walsh, and Raymond Williams—to name but a few—have contained chapters or sections on Lawrence of great interest. To keep track of essays and articles on Lawrence would require a separate publication. And there is no sign that the tide is yet receding.

Leavis' contribution to Lawrence criticism has already been discussed. Among the other postwar books listed above perhaps those by Mark Spilka and Eliseo Vivas may be singled out for further comment, together with *A D. H. Lawrence Miscellany,* as representing certain trends in contemporary criticism of Lawrence.

Spilka declares himself opposed to the custom of dividing Lawrence "into aesthetic and prophetic halves, one of which wrote the good portions of his novels, the other the bad." [19] He wishes, like Forster, to restore the wholeness of Lawrence's work; but, unlike Forster, he is not unable to accept Lawrence's preaching. Spilka is almost a disciple, and his criticism is mainly sympathetic illumination of Lawrence's message—though the message, it must be allowed, is seen as being most fully communicated in the works that are most successful as art. Spilka also stresses Lawrence's "religious dimension"; and the most original chapter in his book is that in which he relates Lawrence's power of creating sudden fourth-dimensional scenes to the primitive religious concept of *mana.*

The weakness of Spilka's mode of criticism is that it leads at times to too close an identification with Lawrence's point of view. In the section on *Sons and Lovers,* for example, Spilka tries to show that Paul Morel is involved in "three destructive forms of love"—in his relations with his mother, with Miriam, and with

Clara. Where Clara and the mother are concerned, Spilka is both sympathetic and critical—just as Lawrence himself is—but in his treatment of Miriam he is most unfair because he accepts Lawrence's surface intention (which is to blame Miriam for the failure of the affair) rather than the whole truth which emerges from the novel in spite of Lawrence himself. *Sons and Lovers* is a better novel than Spilka's criticism would lead us to think because the artist in Lawrence triumphs over the ordinary man.

In *D. H. Lawrence: The failure and the triumph of art* Eliseo Vivas follows the example of Leavis and of Graham Hough (in *The Dark Sun*) by concentrating mainly on Lawrence's artistic achievement. Vivas, unlike Spilka, is not a disciple. Indeed, he is only too clearly in sharp disagreement with Lawrence on many important points, and he allows his own feelings to disturb the detachment which is essential to the aesthetic approach that he avowedly undertakes.

Vivas bases his thesis on Lawrence's own remark in the essay on "The Novel" (in *Reflections on the Death of a Porcupine*): "Oh give me the novel. Let me hear what the novel says. As for the novelist, he is usually a dribbling liar." Just as Blackmur deplores the lack of art in Lawrence's poems, so Vivas finds that in novels—such as *Aaron's Rod, Kangaroo,* and *The Plumed Serpent* —"the artist fails to digest his experience aesthetically." Even in *Sons and Lovers,* in *The Rainbow,* and in *Women in Love,* which are successful as works of art, there is "excess of passion" (Vivas instances the quarrel in Chapter 1 of *Sons and Lovers*); and Lawrence's insistent didacticism intrudes upon the cool restraint that is required of art.

Vivas' most useful contribution is his distinction—again based on a remark by Lawrence himself—between symbolism which is merely a "semiotic sign" and the richer, more mysterious "constitutive symbol" that is exemplified in the highland cattle and rabbit episodes of *Women in Love.* (See above, p. 84.) Lawrence's use of the second kind of symbolism enables him to penetrate to areas of the human psyche unknown to previous novelists; but, for Vivas, it is not the psychological so much as the artistic originality that is impressive.

Several of the essays in *A D. H. Lawrence Miscellany* are also concerned with symbolism—or the allied subject of myth—but in a less philosophical-aesthetic way. The approach of Angelo P. Bertocci, for instance, to "Symbolism in *Women in Love*" is more closely analytical. He is concerned with the effect that Lawrence achieves through a perhaps unconscious network of iterative imagery. This approach—not in Bertocci's essay, but in other contributions to the *Miscellany*—leads to an obsession with symbol hunting that becomes an end in itself; but the inclusion of other essays of a very different kind—such as Raymond Williams' "The Social Thinking of D. H. Lawrence" and Mark Schorer's "Lawrence and the Spirit of Place"—corrects this excess.

What contemporary criticism of Lawrence still most needs is a balanced assessment of the visionary and familiar elements which are both so strongly present in Lawrence's work. Graham Hough has the catholicity of interest necessary to such an approach, and for that reason *The Dark Sun* is the nearest of the books so far published in realizing the ideal, all-round judgment of Lawrence. But Hough writes with the air of a relaxed, intelligent clubman mulling over the work of a wayward genius, and this manner prevents him from attaining either the sympathy of Spilka or the penetration of Vivas in his comments on Lawrence's symbolism.

The best criticism on Lawrence has been concerned with limited portions of his work only. This is not a satisfactory way of dealing with a writer who is so diverse, and sometimes self-contradictory, as Lawrence; but, until the critic comes along who can grasp the whole of the man and the whole of his work, with the right degree of both sympathy and detachment, Lawrence's readers will have to be content with partial illumination.

II *Lawrence's Influence*

Few English or American writers since the 1920's can have failed to be influenced—whether reacting favorably or unfavorably—by D. H. Lawrence. Like Byron, he is also a figure of European importance whose influence has extended far beyond the confines of his own country and language. The present brief discussion will be restricted, however, to Lawrence's influences on English writers and on one or two from the British Commonwealth. To begin with, this influence as might be expected, was greater on the thought and feeling of writers than on their methods of composition. "When I first read Lawrence in the late Twenties," says W. H. Auden, "it was his message which made the greatest impression on me, so that it was his 'think' books like *Fantasia of the Unconscious* rather than his fiction which I read most avidly." [20]

Other young poets in the 1930's continued to be influenced in the same way. They coupled him, as did F. R. Leavis, with Blake—particularly with the Blake who sought to correct the inhibitive reason of eighteenth-century materialist philosophy by emphasizing the neglected forces of passion and imagination. Lawrence's attacks on the tyranny of mental consciousness and his exposure of the sterility of twentieth-century emotional life are echoed in the antisuburban sentiments of the Auden-Mac-Neice-Day Lewis-Spender group of poets; but, of course, their views were colored by political interests which were alien to Lawrence.

Aldous Huxley was similarly influenced by Lawrence's diagnosis of the evils of modern civilization, and he showed his admiration for his friend by introducing him and Frieda into *Point Counter Point* as Mark and Mary Rampion. Huxley presents Mark Rampion as urging the need for "a revolt in favour of life and wholeness"; but Lawrence himself, though he thought highly of *Point Counter Point* as a picture of the young generation to which Huxley belonged, dismissed Rampion as "the most boring character in the book—a gas-bag."

A rather different reaction—and one that suggests the beginning of a deeper and more lasting influence on the imaginations rather than simply the opinions of other writers—is that suggested by Stephen Spender in his autobiography *World Within World*. Spender began to read Lawrence, as did Auden, in the 1920's, while an undergraduate at Oxford. Writers like James Joyce, Proust, and Virginia Woolf had revealed to him how the external world could be turned into a *paysage intérieur*, "an object of interior sensibility." Lawrence challenged the whole character of this type of literature:

Lawrence, despite his artistic defects, wrote poetry and prose which turned outwards from himself towards men and women, and towards nature. He had an abhorrence for the isolation of certain modern writers within their own highly developed sensibility. He had a sense that the distinctions between outer and inner are sacred: that whilst the inner life should meet the outer, the outer world should not become the inner world of the writer. To him the idea of the separateness of perceiving from what is perceived, of man from nature and from other men, is sacred. Meeting is a dark mystery, a kind of godliness, and even within the fusion of the sexual act the separateness of man and woman remain. This paradox of a fusion of existences which cannot become one another is for him the creative mystery. For from the contact of the individual with what is outside him, with nature, and with other people, there is a renewal of himself.[21]

But Lawrence also undermined Spender's confidence in himself. "I felt the force of his criticism of his contemporaries," Spender adds a few sentences later, "and did not feel that I myself was spared his condemnation of Oxford undergraduates and namby-pamby young men."

One of the few novelists of Lawrence's own time to be influenced by him in style as well as content was Richard Aldington. *Death of a Hero* (1929) and *The Colonel's Daughter* (1931) are written in a tumbling, colloquial manner which is very like a crude imitation of the relaxed (often too relaxed) style of *Aaron's Rod* and *Kangaroo*. The first two parts of *Death of a Hero* are an attempt to relate the confusion of the World War I generation in England to the sanctimonious self-deception of their Victorian parents; and the war itself is seen as the explosive culmination of a long process of hypocrisy—a theme perhaps inspired by Lawrence's "England, My England." The general influence of Lawrence's contempt for sterile convention is quite apparent in *Death of a Hero;* and in *The Colonel's Daughter* this aspect of Lawrence's influence is even more obvious. Georgie, the heroine of this second novel, is a completely convention-ridden girl. Lawrence would almost certainly have made her break out of her shell, like Alvina Houghton; but Aldington is interested in the habits of mind that make it impossible for her to do so. Here the two writers part company.

Aldington is not a skillful artist. It is difficult to say whether Lawrence, by sharpening Aldington's sense of the deadness of middle-class society, prompted him to write better novels, or, by offering him the wrong sort of model, blunted the small talent that he had. The impact of Lawrence was probably too great; and the man and all that he stood for were probably too close to Aldington personally for his influence to be one that could fertilize rather than overwhelm Aldington's own minor gift for satirical writing.

On more recent writers Lawrence's influence has been, for the most part, less direct, but perhaps correspondingly more beneficial. To the poets he has given not a new doctrine but a new interest in the exploration of the unconscious by means of symbol and myth. The neo-Romantic poets of the 1940's, Dylan Thomas most notable among them, seem to have felt this influence. The prelapsarian grandeur that attends Lawrence's presentation of "the old agricultural England" in *The Rainbow* can be felt in the poems that Thomas writes about his childhood; and at least one recent poet, Edwin Muir, has written a fine poem ("Horses") which is directly inspired by Lawrence. On the South African poet Roy Campbell and on the Australian Judith Wright, Lawrence's influence can also be detected. The publication of *Kangaroo* and of *The Boy in the Bush* stimulated the desire of Australian poets to write a truly indigenous literature, and the foundation of a new nationalistic literary movement followed. Judith Wright is the finest product of this movement, and some of her excellent animal poems suggest the influence of *Birds, Beasts and Flowers*.

Among novelists, Elizabeth Bowen and Lawrence Durrell may be mentioned as giving evidence of a change in the atmosphere of the modern novel which is at least in part attributable to Lawrence. Elizabeth Bowen writes: "We want the naturalistic surface, but with a kind of internal burning. In Lawrence every bush burns." [22] Many modern novelists, of course, are content with flat naturalism, but on those who try to communicate the full emotional body of experience Lawrence's "constitutive symbolism," although it is extremely difficult to imitate, has had a profound influence. Even so un-Lawrentian a novelist as Iris Murdoch seeks in the major symbolic episodes of her novels to achieve that fusion of naturalism with "a kind of internal burning" which Elizabeth Bowen recognizes as Lawrence's peculiar achievement.

Two recent novels that suggest a specific rather than a general debt to Lawrence are *The Go-Between* (1953) by L. P. Hartley and *The Grass is Singing* (1950) by Doris Lessing. Both novels inevitably call *Lady Chatterley's Lover* to the reader's mind, but that of Doris Lessing is the closer in spirit and in method to Lawrence. *The Grass is Singing* is a study of the decay of a marriage between an ill-matched couple who live on a poverty-stricken, incompetently managed farm on the Rhodesian veld. The sexlessness of their marriage is a parallel to the impotence of Sir Clifford Chatterley, but it has its roots in poverty and deprivation rather than in industrialism and false "liberalism." The black houseboy who becomes the Mellors intruding on this relationship is ambiguously regarded by the white woman. He brings destruction instead of rebirth; and it is not destruction of a cleansing

Lawrentian kind, but the violent culmination of a long, demoralizing process. Yet the peculiar compulsion which the houseboy exerts over the white woman is intensely Lawrentian; and the scene in which the woman accidentally comes upon him when he is washing himself is clearly derived from *Lady Chatterley*. The breaking of the "formal pattern of black-and-white, mistress-and-servant" by "the personal relation"—against all the racial instincts of the woman—is also reminiscent of the way in which Mellors, simply by being what he is, breaks through the class barrier which Connie instinctively raises between them.

L. P. Hartley's *The Go-Between,* on the other hand, is *Lady Chatterley's Lover* strained through the filter of Henry James. Marian, an upper-class girl who carries on an affair with a young farmer, Ted, although she is to marry Lord Trimingham, is the counterpart in this novel of Constance Chatterley. The fact that Lord Trimingham's face has been mutilated in the Boer War suggests a deliberate parallel with Sir Clifford. In character, however, Lord Trimingham is quite different—he is chivalrous and generous, where Clifford is hypocritical and mean. Marian, to match this contrast, lacks the real, natural nobility of Constance, although she is not without warmth of feeling and desire. It is as if Hartley were retelling the Chatterley story from what he considers a more probable point of view. But everything is seen through the eyes of a boy on the verge of adolescence who is a visitor to Brandham Hall and who is used by the lovers as their messenger. This alters the impact of the novel entirely. Its major theme becomes the Jamesian one of innocence encountering and being bewildered by experience.

When at the end Marian—fifty years after Ted has committed suicide—looks back on their love affair and sees it as "a beautiful thing," in contrast with the "denatured humanity" of the twentieth century, the effect is almost that of a parody of Lawrence. Marian is in reality selfish and self-deceived. The final ambiguity of the novel, which contrives to cast doubt on the half-acknowledged values of the first-person narrator, narrows the distance between Hartley and Lawrence, but still leaves a gulf between them.

Lawrence as a working-class writer has had some influence on a group of postwar novelists and playwrights who have tried to present working-class life honestly and from the inside. Alan Sillitoe, John Braine, Arnold Wesker, Shelagh Delaney and, again, Doris Lessing, in such stories as "He" and "The Other Woman," are all general, but not very close derivatives of the Lawrence of *Sons and Lovers*. Only Doris Lessing is akin to him in her method of writing. The chief problem for the working-class writer is that of tone. In a lecture on autobiography entitled "A Question of Tone," Richard Hoggart discusses his own experience of this problem and his realization of the success with which Lawrence solved it in *Sons and Lovers:*

For myself, I have only once or twice and then in very brief passages felt that I was getting into my prose the particular run or rhythm of my own make-up. This is partly, as I have admitted, a problem for any writer at any time, whatever his social background. But just here I am anxious to put the emphasis on the social aspects of this search—that it is easier for certain manners and tones to express themselves, because so much of our writing has traditionally been expressed in those tones of voice. I remember a peculiar excitement when one day I read the opening of *Sons and Lovers*. I had read it many times before; but this time I saw something (or heard something) more in it. In some ways it is not a particularly impressive passage. But I realised now that its movement, its 'kick,' its voice, was that of a working-class man who had become articulate and—instead of acquiring rhythms foreign to his deep-rooted ways of feeling—had kept the rhetoric of his kind and so (this is the point) could better say what *he* had to say at that point.[23]

This particular aspect of Lawrence's writing is not so much an actual as a potential influence. But as the realization of the special difficulties and achievement of Lawrence's tone in *Sons and Lovers* (and, I would add, in his poetry as well) becomes more widespread, it may yet lead to the flourishing of a genuinely inward quality in working-class writing. The honest, but crude observation of the present group of writers on working-class life may be supplemented by a language more adequate to the "deep-rooted ways of feeling" of that class.

III   *Conclusion: Lawrence's Place in English Literature*

Considering that he died at the age of forty-four, the quality and the quantity of Lawrence's writing are astonishing. In creative vitality he must be reckoned on a par with Dickens. Lawrence's range is smaller than that of Dickens, but within his narrower sphere he goes much deeper; and the exuberance that is so characteristic of Dickens, although suggested in *The Lost Girl* and in parts of *Sons and Lovers* and in *The First Lady Chatterley*, is checked in Lawrence by a profound dissatisfaction with English civilization. Between these two writers lies a period of social change which separates the Victorian sensibility from the Modern; and, if Dickens is the novelist supremely representative of the first, Lawrence is the name which most readily springs to mind in connection with the second. Yet they are also related by a continuing tradition. Lawrence was born in the nineteenth century; his mind was fed with nineteenth-century art and ideas; and his innovations, great as they were, did not in the end destroy his nineteenth-century inheritance, but made it relevant to the twentieth century.

A Victorian novelist who is in some ways a more obvious ancestor of Lawrence is George Eliot. They share a similar nonconformist provincial background; and it probably is from George Eliot, more than from any other novelist, that Lawrence draws his strong moral preoccupations. But in George Eliot can be seen at work that intensely self-conscious intellectualizing process which the mature Lawrence resisted so strongly. Her patient, sympathetic, but also laborious, reflectiveness—the quality which makes her the most "serious" of the Victorian novelists—represents an element in the nineteenth-century tradition that was handed on to Lawrence and that weighed down with a heavy burden of "knowledge" his natural, Dickensian spontaneity. That Lawrence became a writer of vivid sensuous immediacy, in spite of this burden, is a tribute to his immense powers of self-transformation. He had to contend with the voices of his "accursed human education" before he could reach the unforced flow of language that he prized.

Lawrence's struggle for spontaneity involved the paradoxically conscious effort to slough off the dead skin of mental consciousness so that a new animal vitality could emerge. Although this metaphor is suggested by Lawrence's favorite symbol, the snake, the animal that Lawrence tried to urge into new life was man— man as fully an animal and therefore as fully himself. There are, one must admit, parts of his work—and perhaps a period of his life—in which he seems to be prepared to jettison the consciously discriminating intellect. "The Woman Who Rode Away" (1928) is his most perfect artistic expression of this impulse; but the tale also contains an implicit recognition of the fallacy inherent in the attempt. The immolation of the woman, which is to be the symbolic climax of the tale, is permanently arrested. Beyond the stroke of the knife there can be nothing recognizably human.

A more complex ideal—and one to which Lawrence returns in his last years—is the theme and standard by which judgments are made in *The Rainbow* and in *Women in Love*. The double symbol of the Brangwen "Marsh" (its reference to the teeming farm life and to the flat, clogging of the spirit) and the restless aspirations—for which sometimes the church and sometimes the bird are a symbol—indicate an unwillingness to be satisfied with anything less than the fullest possible development of the human being. Strong as was Lawrence's yearning for a sense of rooted identity with "great creating nature," encouraged both by his reading and by his own adolescent enthusiasm for the Haggs, he was himself the product of forces which had already gone far toward depriving the working class of vital contact with the soil and toward destroying the rhythms of the "old agricultural England." The intelligence—and the frustrations, too—of his mother did more to detach him from his surroundings and to encourage his natural impatience with mere passive acceptance of the way things are. And in time the growth of his own genius, since it made him see things that other men did not, or would not, see, set him apart from the rest of the world. He became of necessity a self-aware individualist, one who was bound to value the intelligence—even though he found it a dangerous, disruptive force—which guided and formulated his own questioning impulses.

Wholeness of being is Lawrence's great theme, and to have gone at least part of the way towards discovering a mode of writing that would not merely advocate but communicate wholeness is his chief contribution to the English novel. The more particular achievements which have been examined in the earlier chapters of this book—his integration of the Romantics' visionary world with the world of the naturalistic novelist; his revaluation of the concept of "character" (as outlined in the "carbon" letter to Edward Garnett); and his extension of the subject matter of the novel to include an inward portrayal of working-class life, and a serious treatment of man's sexual experience—all these are part of the overriding and unifying theme of wholeness.

Few novelists can have broken so much new ground as Lawrence, and yet he is never what is usually thought of as a literary experimenter. The cast of his mind is entirely different from that,

say, of James Joyce. His innovations grow out of an overwhelming
need to discover the meaning of his own experience. "If you ex-
amine the works of any great innovator," writes T. S. Eliot, "in
chronological order, you may expect to find that the author has
been driven on, step by step, in his innovations, by an inner
necessity, and the novelty of form has rather been forced upon
him by his material than deliberately sought." [24] This statement is
almost, but not quite, applicable to Lawrence. The reluctance to
make changes which Eliot implies and the reduction of the author to the status of impersonal servant of his material are not
characteristic of Lawrence; but the submission to "inner necessity" is. Not that there is an equal intensity and pressure of inner
necessity throughout the whole of his work. As between one work
and another—and as between parts of the same work—he is an
uneven writer. But the distinctively Lawrentian quality that can
be distilled from the whole of his work is one of personal immediacy; it is a refusal to accept something at secondhand, or
through the mediation of external authority, or of convention.
Like his own Ursula in *The Rainbow*, Lawrence is impelled to
find out what life means to him personally. His originality as an
artist is the result of his imagination playing its willing part in
the process of discovery which this sincerity demands. At his
best, Lawrence gives the impression of living right through the
very words he writes, and in this he is inimitable.

Notes and References

Chapter One

1. *The Collected Letters of D. H. Lawrence,* ed. Harry T. Moore (London, 1962), II, 952-53.

2. *Ibid.,* I, 371.

3. *Phoenix,* ed. Edward D. McDonald (London, 1936; reprint, 1961), p. 133.

4. *Ibid.*

5. *Ibid.,* p. 134.

6. *D. H. Lawrence, A Composite Biography,* compiled by Edward Nehls (University of Wisconsin Press, 1957, 1958, 1959), I, 24.

7. *Collected Letters,* II, 1100.

8. *Phoenix,* p. 137.

9. *Ibid.,* p. 139.

10. *Ibid.,* p. 829.

11. Nehls, I, 7. (From L.'s "Autobiographical Sketch.")

12. *Ibid.,* p. 9. (From Ada L.'s *Young Lorenzo.*)

13. *Ibid.,* p. 7. (From L.'s "Autobiographical Sketch.")

14. *Ibid.,* p. 10. (From Ada L.'s *Young Lorenzo.*)

15. *Fantasia of the Unconscious* (New York, 1922; reprint, London, 1933), Chapter VIII, p. 86.

16. *Ibid.,* pp. 89-90.

17. *Ibid.,* Chapter VI, p. 60.

18. *Ibid.,* Chapter V, p. 52.

19. Letter of Frieda Lawrence to Frederick J. Hoffman, Nov. 21, 1942, quoted in "Lawrence's Quarrel with Freud," *The Achievement of D. H. Lawrence,* ed. Frederick J. Hoffman and Harry T. Moore (University of Oklahoma Press, 1953), p. 109.

20. *Collected Letters,* I, 180.

21. *Cf.* "All the animals in Paradise enjoyed the sensual passion of coition." We were driven out, "Not because we sinned, but because we got our sex into our head," *Fantasia,* Chapter VII, p. 76.

22. *Studies in Classic American Literature* (New York, 1923; Anchor Books edition, New York, 1951), Chapter 1, p. 17.

23. "The Spinner and the Monks," *Twilight in Italy* (London, 1916; Penguin edition, 1960), p. 31.

24. "The Lemon Gardens," *op. cit.*, p. 60.

25. "The Crucifix Across the Mountains," *op. cit.*, p. 11.

26. "The Mozo," *Mornings in Mexico* (London, 1927; edition printed with *Etruscan Places*, London, 1956), p. 23.

27. "The Hopi Snake Dance," *op. cit.*, p. 67.

28. *Phoenix*, p. 99.

29. "The Painted Tombs of Tarquinia," *Etruscan Places* (London, 1932; edition printed with *Mornings in Mexico*, London, 1956), I, 49.

30. *A D. H. Lawrence Miscellany*, ed. Harry T. Moore (Southern Illinois University Press, 1959), pp. 326-40.

31. A. W. McLeod in a note written for Harry T. Moore's *The Intelligent Heart* (New York, 1955; revised edition, Penguin Books, London, 1960), p. 112. (Nehls, I, 90.)

32. Nehls, I, 116. (From Ford's *Portraits from Life*.)

33. Wordsworth, *The Prelude*, I, 393. *Cf.* Aldous Huxley: "Lawrence's special and characteristic gift was an extraordinary sensitiveness to what Wordsworth called 'unknown modes of being.' He was always intensely aware of the mystery of the world, and the mystery was always for him a *numen*, divine." (Introduction to *Letters*, London, 1932, pp. xi-xii.)

34. *Phoenix*, pp. 532, 537.

35. *Ibid.*, p. 528.

36. "Foreword' to Fr. William Tiverton's *D. H. Lawrence and Human Existence* (London, 1951).

37. *Collected Letters*, I, 273.

Chapter Two

1. Preface to *Lyrical Ballads* (1802).

2. *Collected Letters*, I, p. 19.

3. The passage to which this refers comes from Lawrence's Author's Note to *The Collected Poems* (London, 1928), reprinted at the beginning of the first volume of *The Complete Poems* (London, 1957). The relevant sentences are quoted in Chapter 8 of the present study (p. 180).

4. *Collected Letters*, I, 93, 94.

5. Dorothy van Ghent, *The English Novel: Form and Function* (New York, 1953; reprint, 1961), p. 253.

6. *Collected Letters*, I, 66-67. Lawrence actually refers to *Paul Morel*, which was his earlier title for *Sons and Lovers*.

7. Graham Hough, *The Dark Sun* (London, 1956; Penguin edition, London, 1961), p. 57.

Chapter Three

1. F. R. Leavis, *D. H. Lawrence, Novelist* (London, 1955), pp. 144-45.

2. Patricia Abel and Robert Hogan, "D. H. Lawrence's Singing Birds" (*A D. H. Lawrence Miscellany,* pp. 204-14). Their comment arises out of an article by E. L. Nicholes, "The Simile of the Sparrow in *The Rainbow,*" *Modern Language Notes* (March, 1949), pp. 171-74; reprinted in *The Achievement of D. H. Lawrence,* pp. 159-62).

3. *Fantasia of the Unconscious,* Chapter XIV, pp. 154-55.

Chapter Four

1. Eliseo Vivas, *D. H. Lawrence: The failure and the triumph of art* (Northwestern University Press, 1960), p. 245.

Chapter Five

1. F. R. Leavis, *op. cit.,* p. 32.

2. Chapter XI, p. 123: "And to have one's own 'gentle spouse' by one's side, of course, to dig one in the ribs occasionally."

3. Graham Hough, *The Dark Sun,* Penguin edition, p. 120.

4. This section is taken from a somewhat longer article by the present author: "Authority and the Individual: A Study of D. H. Lawrence's *Kangaroo,*" *The Critical Quaterly* (Autumn, 1959).

5. Lawrence's description of the *Bulletin* at the beginning of Chapter 14 is accurate. Some of the "bits" in this chapter come straight from the June, 1922, issues of the *Bulletin.* The story of the kangaroo and the wildcat is from June 8, and the bullocks drowning in Gippsland is from the June 22 issue. Many of the subjects covered by the Diggers at their debates and discussions are also reminiscent of the titles of *Bulletin* leaders.

Chapter Six

1. *Collected Letters,* I, 845. *Cf.* also pp. 844, 859.

2. *Phoenix,* p. 147.

3. *The Dark Sun,* p. 150.

4. Jascha Kessler: "Descent in Darkness: The Myth of *The Plumed Serpent,*" *A D. H. Lawrence Miscellany,* pp. 239-61.

5. W. Y. Tindall connects this phrase with Madame Blavatsky. See his *D. H. Lawrence and Susan His Cow* (Columbia University Press, 1939). The relevant chapter is reprinted in *The Achievement of D. H. Lawrence,* pp. 178-84.

6. By Edmund Wilson in a brilliant review of *Lady Chatterley* in the *New Republic,* July 3, 1929 (reprinted in *The Achievement of D. H. Lawrence,* pp. 185-88); by Graham Hough in the section on *Lady Chatterley* in *The Dark Sun;* and by Richard Hoggart in his Introduction to the Penguin Books, *second* (not in the first) edition of the novel, London, 1961. See also *The Trial of Lady Chatterley,* edited by C. H. Rolph (Penguin Books, London, 1961).

7. "À Propos of *Lady Chatterley's Lover*" (London, 1930; reprinted Penguin Books, London, 1961), p. 124.

8. Introduction to Penguin edition of *Lady Chatterley* (second edition, London, 1961), p. viii.

Chapter Seven

1. Quoted in Harry T. Moore, *The Intelligent Heart* (New York, 1955; revised edition, Penguin Books, London, 1960), p. 106.
2. Ford Madox Ford. (Nehls, I, 108, from *Portraits from Life.*)

Chapter Eight

1. *D. H. Lawrence: Selected Poems,* ed. W. E. Williams (Penguin Books, London, 1950), Introduction, p. 7.
2. Introduction to *New Poems* (American edition, New York, 1920), reprinted in *D. H. Lawrence: Selected Literary Criticism,* ed. Anthony Beal (Mercury Books, London, 1961), pp. 84-89.
3. See *The Double Agent* (New York, 1935). Also *Language as Gesture* (London, 1954). There is an interesting discussion, and refutation, of Blackmur's views by Professor Pinto in *The Critical Quarterly* (Spring, 1961). Professor Pinto's essay, "Poet Without a Mask," is an excellent study of Lawrence's poetry in general. (See also Christopher Hassall: "D. H. Lawrence and the Etruscans," *Essays by Divers Hands,* London, 1962.)
4. The phrase "artifice of eternity" comes from Yeats' "Sailing to Byzantium," line 24.
5. Author's Note to *The Collected Poems* (London, 1928), reprinted as *The Complete Poems* (London, 1957), I, xxxvi.
6. Harry T. Moore: *The Life and Works of D. H. Lawrence* (New York, 1951), p. 77.
7. "Note," *The Complete Poems* (London, 1957), III, xl.
8. *Fire-Bird* (London, 1951), pp. 32-33.
9. *Cf.* Yeats' poem "The Tower."
10. *Etruscan Places* (London, 1956 ed.), Chapter III, p. 42.
11. *Apocalypse* (Florence, 1931; Albatross Modern Continental Library edition, Hamburg, 1932), XVI, pp. 176-77.
12. *Etruscan Places,* Chapter I, p. 10.
13. *Ibid.,* p. 12.

Chapter Nine

1. *Faith that Illuminates,* 1935. Reprinted in *T. S. Eliot, Selected Prose,* ed. John Hayward (Penguin Books, London, 1953).
2. *After Strange Gods* (New York, 1934), p. 66.
3. *Ibid.,* p. 53.
4. Eliot may have changed his attitude toward Lawrence in recent years. Although his Foreword to Father William Tiverton's *D. H. Lawrence and Human Existence* (London, 1951) does not show much change of opinion, the fact of his writing it is perhaps significant. In

"American Literature and the American Language," an address given at Washington University in 1953, Eliot is complimentary about *Studies in Classic American Literature,* and I am given to understand that at the *Lady Chatterley* trial in 1960 he made it known that if the prosecution were to quote from *After Strange Gods* he would testify for the defense. How much can be read into details such as these I do not know, but they certainly suggest that Eliot is now rather more sympathetic toward Lawrence than he was in the 1920's and 1930's.

5. "I have trifled with the exordia" is a phrase of James' reported by Edith Wharton in *A Backward Glance* (New York, 1934). The other phrase is from *Notes on Novelists* (London, 1914) by James himself. I am indebted for both references to Armin Arnold's *D. H. Lawrence and America.*

6. "D. H. Lawrence's Delusion," *The Evening Standard,* April 10, 1930. (Quoted Armin Arnold, p. 179.)

7. Letter to *The Nation and the Athenaeum,* April 26, 1930.

8. *The Letters of D. H. Lawrence* (London, 1932), p. x.

9. *For Continuity* (Cambridge, England, 1933), p. 111.

10. *Ibid.,* pp. 114 and 117.

11. *Ibid.,* p. 117.

12. *Ibid.,* pp. 130 and 131.

13. *Ibid.,* p. 123.

14. *D. H. Lawrence, Novelist* (London, 1955), p. 17.

15. *Ibid.,* p. 15.

16. *Studies in a Dying Culture* (London, 1938; reprint of 1948), pp. 56-57.

17. *The Double Agent* (New York, 1935); reprinted in *Language as Gesture* (London, 1954). Quotations from latter edition, pp. 287 and 300.

18. *The Shaping Spirit* (London, 1958; Grey Arrow reprint, 1963), p. 142.

19. *The Love Ethic of D. H. Lawrence* (Indiana University Press, 1955; reprint of 1959), p. 3.

20. *The Dyer's Hand* (London, 1963), p. 278.

21. *World Within World* (London, 1951), p. 97.

22. Quoted by Mark Schorer in "Technique as Discovery" (*Forms of Modern Fiction,* edited by William van O'Connor, University of Minnesota Press, 1948; reprint by Indiana University Press, 1959), p. 29.

23. *The Critical Quarterly* (Spring, 1963), p. 89.

24. *After Strange Gods,* p. 25.

Selected Bibliography

PRIMARY SOURCES

(For greater detail see Roberts, Warren. *A Bibliography of D. H. Lawrence*. London, Rupert Hart-Davis, 1963 and Nehls, I, 527-31.

The White Peacock. London, Heinemann, 1911.
The Trespasser. London, Duckworth, 1912.
Love Poems and Others. London, Duckworth, 1913.
Sons and Lovers. London, Duckworth, 1913.
The Widowing of Mrs. Holroyd. London, Duckworth, 1914.
The Prussian Officer and Other Stories. London, Duckworth, 1914.
The Rainbow. London, Methuen, 1915.
Twilight in Italy. London, Duckworth, 1916.
Amores. London, Duckworth, 1916.
Look! We Have Come Through! London, Chatto and Windus, 1917.
New Poems. London, Martin Secker, 1918.
Bay: A Book of Poems. London, The Beaumont Press, 1919.
Touch and Go. London, C. W. Daniel, 1920.
Women in Love. New York, Privately Printed for Subscribers Only, 1920. London, Martin Secker, 1921.
The Lost Girl. London, Martin Secker, 1920.
Psychoanalysis and the Unconscious. New York, Thomas Seltzer, 1921.
Movements in European History (by "Lawrence H. Davison"). London, Oxford University Press, 1921.
Tortoises. New York, Thomas Seltzer, 1921.
Sea and Sardinia. New York, Thomas Seltzer, 1921.
Aaron's Rod. New York, Thomas Seltzer, 1922.
Fantasia of the Unconscious. New York, Thomas Seltzer, 1922.
England, My England and Other Stories. New York, Thomas Seltzer, 1922.
The Ladybird. London, Martin Secker, 1923. (Contains "The Ladybird," "The Fox," and "The Captain's Doll.") Published in America under the title *The Captain's Doll*. New York, Thomas Seltzer, 1923.
Studies in Classic American Literature. New York, Thomas Seltzer, 1923.
Kangaroo. London, Martin Secker, 1923.
Birds, Beasts and Flowers. New York, Thomas Seltzer, 1923.
The Boy in the Bush. With M. L. Skinner. London, Martin Secker, 1924.
St. Mawr: Together with The Princess. London, Martin Secker, 1925.
Reflections on the Death of a Porcupine and Other Essays. Philadelphia, The Centaur Press, 1925.
The Plumed Serpent (*Quetzalcoatl*). London, Martin Secker, 1926.
David. London, Martin Secker, 1926.

Sun. London, E. Archer, 1926. Unexpurgated edition, Paris, The Black Sun Press, 1928.

Glad Ghosts. London, Benn, 1926.

Mornings in Mexico. London, Martin Secker, 1927.

Rawdon's Roof. London, Elkin Mathews and Marrot, 1928.

The Woman Who Rode Away and Other Stories. London, Martin Secker, 1928. American edition includes "The Man Who Loved Islands." New York, Knopf, 1928.

Lady Chatterley's Lover. Florence, Privately Printed, 1928.

The Collected Poems of D. H. Lawrence. 2 vols. London, Martin Secker, 1928.

Cavalleria Rusticana and Other Stories. Translated from the Italian of Giovanni Verga, London, Jonathan Cape, 1928.

The Paintings of D. H. Lawrence. Introduction by Lawrence. London, The Mandrake Press, 1929.

Pansies. London, Martin Secker, 1929.

My Skirmish with Jolly Roger. New York, Random House, 1929.

The Escaped Cock. Paris, The Black Sun Press, 1929. With the title *The Man Who Died,* London, Martin Secker, 1931.

Pornography and Obscenity. London, Faber and Faber, 1929.

Nettles. London, Faber and Faber, 1930.

Assorted Articles. London, Martin Secker, 1930.

The Virgin and the Gipsy. Florence, G. Orioli, 1930.

À Propos of Lady Chatterley's Lover. London, The Mandrake Press, 1930.

The Triumph of the Machine. London, Faber and Faber, 1930.

Love Among the Haystacks and Other Pieces. London, The Nonesuch Press, 1930.

Apocalypse. Florence, G. Orioli, 1931.

The Letters of D. H. Lawrence. Ed. Aldous Huxley. London, Heinemann, 1932.

Last Poems. Florence, G. Orioli, 1932.

Etruscan Places. London, Martin Secker, 1932.

The Lovely Lady and Other Stories. London, Martin Secker, 1933.

The Plays of D. H. Lawrence. London, Martin Secker, 1933.

A Collier's Friday Night. London, Martin Secker, 1934.

The Tales of D. H. Lawrence. London, Martin Secker, 1934.

A Modern Lover (includes the unfinished novel, *Mr. Noon*). London, Martin Secker, 1934.

Phoenix: The Posthumous Papers of D. H. Lawrence. London, Heinemann, 1936.

The First Lady Chatterley. New York, The Dial Press, 1944.

D. H. Lawrence's Letters to Bertrand Russell. Ed. Harry T. Moore. New York, Gotham Book Mart, 1948.

The Complete Poems of D. H. Lawrence. 3 vols. London, Heinemann, 1957.

Selected Bibliography

The Symbolic Meaning: The Uncollected Versions of Studies in Classic American Literature. Ed. Armin Arnold. Fontwell, Arundel, The Centaur Press, 1962.

The Collected Letters of D. H. Lawrence. 2 vols. Ed. Harry T. Moore. London, Heinemann, 1962.

The Complete Poems of D. H. Lawrence. Collected and Edited with an Introduction by Vivian de Sola Pinto and Warren Roberts. 2 vols. London, Heinemann, 1964.

SECONDARY SOURCES

A. Biography and Memoirs

Aldington, Richard. D. H. Lawrence. London, Chatto and Windus, 1930.

———. Portrait of a Genius But. . . . London, Heinemann, 1950. First attempt by someone who knew Lawrence well to write a reasonably detached life and critique of the work. Title indicates its approach.

Brewster, Earl and Achsah. D. H. Lawrence, Reminiscences and Correspondence. London, Martin Secker, 1934. Sane. Casts light on Lawrence's interest in Buddhism and the Etruscans. Contains a number of letters.

Bynner, Witter. Journey with Genius, Recollections and Reflections Concerning the D. H. Lawrences. New York, John Day, 1951. Friend of the Lawrences when they first visited Mexico.

Carswell, Catherine. The Savage Pilgrimage. London, Chatto and Windus, 1932. Very pro-Lawrence. "Here is a man who lived from a pure source and steadfastly refused to break faith with that source."

Carter, Frederick. D. H. Lawrence and the Body Mystical. London, Denis Archer, 1932. This book contains useful clues to the "mysticism" in The Plumed Serpent and Apocalypse. (Lawrence's Apocalypse was originally meant as an introduction to a book by Carter.)

E. T. [Jessie (Chambers) Wood]. D. H. Lawrence, A Personal Record. London, Jonathan Cape, 1935. By the "Miriam" of Sons and Lovers. Invaluable material about the young Nottinghamshire Lawrence. Unfortunately, Mrs. Wood cannot take a detached view of Sons and Lovers. To her, it is history rather than fictionalized autobiography, and she is also very much concerned with correcting what she regards as the travesty of herself as Miriam.

Lawrence, Ada and Gelder, G. Stuart. Young Lorenzo, Early Life of D. H. Lawrence. Florence, G. Orioli, 1931. Recollections of the early Lawrence by Lawrence's sister.

Lawrence, Frieda. Not I, But the Wind. New York, Viking Press, 1934.

Freshly written, fascinating glimpses of Lawrence and of their life together, by the woman he met in 1912 and eloped with. Also useful insights into the nature of the woman who so profoundly influenced Lawrence's ideas about woman.

Luhan, Mabel Dodge. *Lorenzo in Taos.* New York, Knopf, 1932. By the somewhat eccentric woman who invited Lawrence to America.

Moore, Harry T. *The Life and Works of D. H. Lawrence.* London, Allen and Unwin, 1951. (See revised edition, *D. H. Lawrence: His Life and Works,* in B. *Criticism* below.)

————. *The Intelligent Heart: The Story of D. H. Lawrence.* New York, Farrar, Straus and Young, 1955. (Revised edition, London, Penguin Books, 1960.) By far the best biography of Lawrence; well written, packed with detail.

Nehls, Edward. *D. H. Lawrence, A Composite Biography.* 3 vols. Madison, University of Wisconsin Press, 1957, 1958, 1959. Extremely useful collection of material on Lawrence's life by people who knew him (including extracts from reminiscences published separately) and by Lawrence himself.

B. *Criticism*

Auden, W. H. *The Dyer's Hand and Other Essays.* London, Faber and Faber, 1963. Contains an interesting essay on the poetry. In the early poems Auden is struck "by the originality of the sensibility and the conventionality of the expressive means." Finds that Lawrence is at his best on nonhuman subjects and that the most interesting of the later verse belongs to a literary genre which Auden calls "satirical doggerel."

Alvarez, A. *The Shaping Spirit.* London, Chatto and Windus, 1958. Contains the best essay so far written on Lawrence's poetry: ". . . a complete truth to feeling. Lawrence is the foremost emotional realist of the century."

Arnold, Armin. *D. H. Lawrence and America.* London, The Linden Press, 1958. Account of Lawrence's connections with America and of the different versions of *Studies in Classic American Literature.* Also useful year-by-year account of Lawrence criticism up to 1958.

Bantock, G. H. *Freedom and Authority in Education.* London, Faber and Faber, 1952. Contains an interesting chapter on Lawrence's educational ideas, prefaced by a résumé of his "philosophy" which brings out Lawrence's emphasis on order.

Beal, Anthony. *D. H. Lawrence.* Edinburgh, Writers and Critics Series, Oliver and Boyd, 1961. Brief survey of Lawrence's work, mainly the novels. Short chapter on "Lawrence's Reputation and Critics." Sensible.

Blackmur, R. P. *The Double Agent.* New York, Arrow Editions, 1935.

Contains Blackmur's attack on Lawrence's poetry as lacking art. (See also *Language as Gesture*. London, Allen and Unwin, 1954.)

Caudwell, Christopher [Christopher Sprigge]. *Studies in a Dying Culture*. London, John Lane, 1938. Essay on Lawrence from Marxist point of view.

Eliot, T. S. *After Strange Gods: A Primer of Modern Heresy*. New York, Harcourt, Brace and Co., 1934. Contains the attack on Lawrence discussed above, pp. 161-62.

Forster, E. M. *Aspects of the Novel*. London, Edward Arnold, 1927. Lawrence presented as a novelist of "prophecy."

Ghent, Dorothy van. *The English Novel: Form and Function*. New York, Rinehart & Company, 1953; reprinted by Harper, 1961. Contains interesting chapter on *Sons and Lovers*.

Hoggart, Richard. Introduction. *Lady Chatterley's Lover*. London, Penguin Books, second edition only, 1961. Clearest defense of *Lady Chatterley* against charge of obscenity. (See also Rolph, editor.)

Hough, Graham. *The Dark Sun, A Study of D. H. Lawrence*. London, Duckworth, 1956. Well-balanced critical survey of all Lawrence's work, including a chapter on "The Doctrine." Clear, humane, pleasantly written; but a little too relaxed and condescending.

Kenmare, Dallas. *Fire-Bird, A Study of D. H. Lawrence*. London, James Barrie, 1951. A study of the poems only. Makes Lawrence seem too much like Shelley.

Kettle, Arnold. *An Introduction to the English Novel*. Vol. II. London, Hutchinson's University Library, 1953. Contains a fairly good chapter on *The Rainbow*.

Leavis, F. R. *D. H. Lawrence*. Cambridge, Minority Press, 1930. Reprinted with slight additions in *For Continuity*, Cambridge, Minority Press, 1933.

———. *D. H. Lawrence, Novelist*. London, Chatto and Windus, 1955. The most outstanding English critic of Lawrence. The 1930 essay, though stimulating, is unsound in its judgment of Lawrence's novels. The later book concentrates on Lawrence's art in the novels—principally *The Rainbow* and *Women in Love* —and in the tales. Takes an unusually admiring view of *St. Mawr*. Rather disappointing on *Sons and Lovers*.

Moore, Harry T. *The Achievement of D. H. Lawrence*. Edited in collaboration with F. J. Hoffman. Norman, University of Oklahoma Press, 1953.

———. *D. H. Lawrence: His Life and Works*. New York, Twayne Publishers, 1964. (Revised edition of *The Life and Works of D. H. Lawrence*, New York, Twayne Publishers, 1951, and London, Allen and Unwin, 1951.) Although some biographical information is provided, this is mainly a study of Lawrence's writings. Frequent direct quotes allow Lawrence, as often as possible, to speak for himself.

——. *A D. H. Lawrence Miscellany*. Carbondale, Southern Illinois University Press, 1959. Both very useful symposia, mainly of critical articles and chapters from books. *The Achievement* has an Introduction on "D. H. Lawrence and His Critics" which surveys criticism and memoirs up to 1953.

Moynahan, Julian. *The Deed of Life*. Princeton, Princeton University Press, 1963. Traces in the fiction a theme of salvation by the "grace" of a greater-than-human force of Life, although this is worked out in terms of an intelligent discussion of Lawrence's *art*. Contains an unusual interpretation of *The Lost Girl*—a novel which Moynahan somewhat overvalues—but is best on the tales.

Murry, John Middleton. *Son of Woman*. London, Jonathan Cape, 1931. Described by Huxley as a "curious essay in destructive hagiography." In Murry's view, Lawrence never shook off the domination of his mother and this distorted his whole treatment of sex and invalidated his art.

Nin, Anais. *D. H. Lawrence: An Unprofessional Study*. Paris, E. W. Titmus, 1932. Contains some interesting insights, but disconnected and abrupt.

Pinto, Vivian De Sola. *D. H. Lawrence, Prophet of the Midlands*. Nottingham, printed by Sisson and Parker, Nottingham for the University of Nottingham, 1952. Public lecture delivered by the head of the English Department at Lawrence's own university.

Potter, Stephen. *D. H. Lawrence: A First Study*. London, Jonathan Cape, 1930. A pioneer study still interesting for its description of certain qualities of Lawrence's writing.

Rolph, C. H. (editor). *The Trial of Lady Chatterley*. London, Penguin Books, 1961. Proceedings of the trial of October 20-November 2, 1960, at the Old Bailey, London, when Penguin Books was prosecuted for allegedly publishing an obscene book (*Lady Chatterley*), but found not guilty. A novel feature of the trial was the admission for the first time in England of evidence as to the literary value of the book under discussion. Several distinguished witnesses, whose testimonies are recorded in this book, were called by the defense.

Schorer, Mark. Introduction. *Lady Chatterley's Lover*. New York, Grove Press, 1957. Reprinted in *"A Propos of Lady Chatterley's Lover" and Other Essays*. London, Penguin Books, 1951. Relates *Lady Chatterley* to the rest of Lawrence's work and discusses the three versions. Other interesting essays by Schorer are included in *Forms of Modern Fiction*, ed. William van O'Connor, University of Minnesota Press, 1948 ("Technique as Discovery"); *The Achievement of D. H. Lawrence*, ed. Harry T. Moore, *q.v.* ("Women in Love") and *A D. H. Lawrence Miscellany*, ed.

Selected Bibliography

Harry T. Moore, *q.v.* ("Lawrence and the Spirit of Place").

Seligmann, Herbert J. *D. H. Lawrence, An American Interpretation.* New York, Thomas Seltzer, 1924. A surprisingly perceptive first study. (See above, p. 163.)

Spender, Stephen. *World Within World.* London, Hamish Hamilton, 1951. Contains interesting passage on Lawrence. (See above, p. 170.)

Spilka, Mark. *The Love Ethic of D. H. Lawrence.* Bloomington, Indiana University Press, 1955. Good sympathetic account of Lawrence's "message," but with emphasis on its expression through art. (See above, pp. 167-68.)

Stewart, J. I. M. *Eight Modern Writers.* Oxford, Oxford University Press, 1963. Contains an extended consideration of Lawrence (109 pages). Written in a somewhat mannered prose, but is in many places very perceptive and, despite a habit of mockery, sympathetic. Particularly good on *The White Peacock, Women in Love, Kangaroo,* and *The Plumed Serpent.*

Tindall, W. Y. *D. H. Lawrence and Susan His Cow.* New York, Columbia University Press, 1939. Witty at Lawrence's expense, but cool, scholarly examination of Lawrence's sources. Thinks *The Plumed Serpent* Lawrence's best novel.

Tiverton, Father William [W. R. Jarrett-Kerr]. *D. H. Lawrence and Human Existence.* London, Rockliff, 1951. Foreword by T. S. Eliot. Tiverton praises Lawrence's criticism; sees connections with Existentialism; and thinks Christians have something to learn from Lawrence.

Vivas, Eliseo. *D. H. Lawrence: The failure and the triumph of art.* Evanston, Northwestern University Press, 1960. Distinguishes between the failures (*Aaron's Rod, Kangaroo, The Plumed Serpent,* and *Lady Chatterley*) and the triumphs (*Sons and Lovers, The Rainbow,* and *Women in Love*) on aesthetic grounds. Carping, but good on Lawrence's use of symbol. (See above, p. 168.)

Walsh, William. *The Use of the Imagination: Educational Thought and the Literary Mind.* London, Chatto and Windus, 1959. Interesting chapters on "The Writer and the Child" which includes discussion of Ursula in *The Rainbow* and "The Writer as Teacher: The Educational Ideas of D. H. Lawrence."

West, Anthony. *D. H. Lawrence.* London, English Novelists Series, Arthur Baker, 1950. Half biography. Thinks well of the tales but not of the novels.

Williams, Raymond. *Culture and Society 1780-1950.* London, Chatto and Windus, 1958. Contains an interesting chapter on Lawrence as a social thinker.

Young, Kenneth. *D. H. Lawrence.* London, British Council pamphlet, Longmans, Green and Co., 1952. Very brief survey. Useful bibliography.

Index

(*References to Lawrence's works will be found under the author's name. The letter* L *is used as an abbreviated form for Lawrence.*)

Index

Index